The Fight To Cure Cancer-

Top Cancer Biotechnology Stocks For Next Five Years

Bhavneesh Sharma, M.D., M.B.A.

Vasuda Capital Management

Andover, Massachusetts

Vasuda Capital Management, LLC
135 North Street
Andover, Massachusetts 01810
www.vasudacapitalmanagement.com

Ordering Information:
Quantity sales. Special discounts are available on quantity purchases by corporations, associations, and others. For details, contact the "Special Sales Department" at the address above.

The Fight To Cure Cancer: Top Cancer Stocks For Next Five Years / Bhavneesh Sharma. —1st ed.

ISBN-13: 978-1517247997

Contents

Dedicated to my wife Manisha and son Bhavya

'Immune manipulation may turn out to be an even more important intervention than chemotherapy was – maybe the most important ever.'

— Roger Perlmutter, president of research at Merck.

CHAPTER 1

The Golden Age of Biotechnology

The DNA was discovered in 1953 and since then there have been tremendous advances in the field of biotechnology, which involves molecular and genetic manipulation to achieve cure to a disease.

In the 1980s the US Supreme Court ruled to allow two bit and genetically modified life-forms. This was perhaps the biggest development in the biotechnology field as far as investors go since this allowed patent protection that is a hallmark of the industry. Patented biotech drugs enjoy a 12-year period of protection from generic competition, allowing a sustained period of favorable returns.

Biotech drugs are expensive, however, and there is pressure from insurers, governments, and consumers to rein in healthcare costs. Some legislators regularly attempt to increase industry competition. If the period of market exclusivity is ever reduced, research-funding sources likely would be curtailed, and there would be a material, negative impact on long-term sales and profitability.

So far, the companies have held on to the prohibition period by successfully arguing that biotech drugs are scientifically complex, not easy to duplicate, and costly to develop.

The biotechnology industry is by far the most research-intensive industry in the U.S. Average R&D intensity (R&D spending to total firm assets) for this industry was 38 percent compared to an average of only about 3 percent for all industries.[1] Biotech firms must determine the best use of cash sourced from operations, as well as from equity and debt issues. First and foremost, the goal is to achieve outsized growth, and managers work to ensure fully funded research and development budgets. Substantial capital is also spent on gaining approval of new drugs and bringing them to full production. Marketing and distribution require sizable funds, as well. Acquisitions are more common among large industry players, which, at times, seek to bolster their lineups. In descending order, debt retirements, stock repurchases, and dividends are the least desirable uses of cash.

By some estimates, only 1 out of every 10,000 investigational new drugs (INDs), which are new molecules at the earliest stages of drug research, ever make it to the market adding a risk associated with R&D to the biotechnology industry.[2]

Biotechnology firms, which are usually small and young without positive earnings, rely on financing from secondary resources like equity financing or partnering with larger pharmaceutical companies. Because sales are sparse for most biotechnology firms, net income is usually low or negative. Biotechnology firms rely partly on partnerships and milestone payments, often from pharmaceutical companies for income. Due to higher cost of capital, these biotechnology companies often face a higher hurdle rate on their R&D projects. In addition, since the stock price of a young biotech company is an expectation of future earnings due to its R&D projects, any significant change in the policy or regulations has a significant effect on the stock price of these companies.

On the other hand, larger pharmaceutical companies with several marketed products and a steady flow of net income and cash spend on an average 25% on R&D and the most of these companies have been buying back stock and retiring debt. Aided by ample cash, large pharmaceutical companies often seek to acquire promising young biotechnology companies to diversify and expand their product pipeline.

CHAPTER 2

Evaluating a public biotechnology company

Using the discounted cash flow method to analyze a biotechnology company is tricky. Most young biotechnology companies do not have a marketed product and no positive earnings. The evaluation of a biotechnology company depends on the products in its research and development pipeline. An analyst needs to look at the disease that drugs in the product pipeline intend to target and how large the market is. An ongoing analysis of the competitive landscape is also important. Companies that are developing drugs that treat the disease or condition with unmet demand are valued higher than those working to develop a vaccine, which is a one-time shot.

Since the results of a single clinical trial can either make or break a young biotechnology company without a marketed product, a company with several products in development would be considered safer.

An experienced researcher can get a fair idea about the chances of success of an ongoing clinical trial by looking at the statistical data of earlier stage clinical trials.

Many small biotechnology companies also need lot of cash to spend on the clinical trials, which involve millions of dollars. To get ongoing cash and royalties and assistance in the FDA approval process, many small biotechnology companies partner with larger pharmaceutical and biotechnology companies. An analyst would consider this a positive sign. A company with ample cash on its balance sheet to spend on the ongoing clinical trials would have less need to do is further financing by diluting shares and would get a higher rank from an analyst.

An experienced management team with the background and management and research and development would further add to the safety factor to consider by analyzing a biotechnology company.

The nature of the operations of firms in the biotechnology Industry makes these equities more suited to aggressive, risk-tolerant investors. Stock prices here can fluctuate dramatically, particularly in response to news developments concerning the success or failure of a particular drug. Investors must carefully consider a stock's risk/reward relationship. Often, investors must be patient and willing to endure years of losses before the benefits of a drug pipeline, in the form of long-term share-price appreciation, are realized.

Understanding the path to getting FDA approval for a drug:

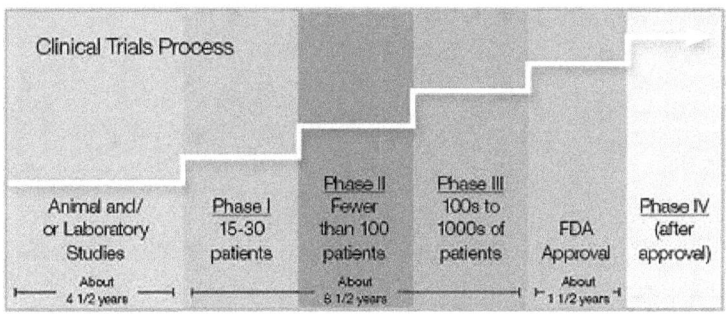

(Image from MD Anderson Cancer Center website)[3]

Phase I trials test if a new treatment is safe and look for the best route (oral/intravenous etc.) to give the treatment. Phase II trials test if the drug is effective in a disease. Usually, the number of patients under study is less than 100. If the treatment is effective, the drug is advanced to larger, controlled phase 3 trials. Phase III trials are done to further confirm the findings of the phase 2 trials in a larger, multicenter (or multinational) patient population, which is compared with a control group (which does not receive the drug). If the drug is effective in phase 3 clinical trials, the drug is filed for approval by the U.S. Food and Drug Administration (F.D.A.). Phase IV trials are done after the drug is approved by the F.D.A. and are done to further study long-term benefits and side effects.

CHAPTER 3

Immunotherapy: The Revolution in Cancer Therapy

Immunotherapy is using the body's immune system to fight cancer cells.

Antibodies:

Antibodies (proteins produced by the body against a target antigen on a cell) are the most successful immunotherapy. Antibodies targeting cancer cell surface receptors like CD20 have been developed and are in clinical use. Once bound to its target, antibodies can induce cancer cell death by various mechanisms. Multiple antibodies are approved to treat cancer, like Rituximab. Immune checkpoint inhibitors, which have shown significant results in clinical studies also fall under this category of cancer immunotherapy.

Immune checkpoint inhibitors:

In normal physiology, **programmed cell death protein**, PD-L1 on the cell surface binds to its ligand, PD-1 on an immune cell surface, which inhibits immune cell activity. Up-regulation of PD-L1 on the cancer cell surface seems to allow them to evade the host immune system by inhibiting T cells that might otherwise attack the tumor cell. Antibodies that bind to either PD-1 or PD-L1 may thus enable T-cells to recognize and attack the tumor cells. Drugs that inhibit these receptors have shown promise in malignant melanoma and non-small cell lung cancer. Drugs inhibiting CTLA4, another immune checkpoint have also shown encouraging results in malignant melanoma. Drugs targeting several other immune-checkpoints are in development. None of the public companies with products in this category made our select list. I believe that the upside in these companies over next 3-5 years is limited to 20-25 percent and this did not meet our cut-off of at least 50 percent upside from current stock price.

Tumor Immunology and PD-1 and PD-L1 pathway[4]

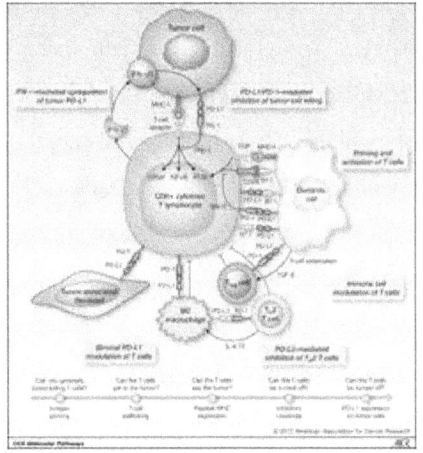

Cytokines:

Cytokines are proteins that regulate the body's immune system. Cytokines like Interferon-alpha are being used in the treatment of cancers like chronic myeloid leukemia.

Cellular therapies:

Cellular therapies, also known as cancer vaccines, involve the removal of immune cells like T cells, natural killer (NK) cells and dendritic cells usually from the patient with the cancer. These immune cells are activated, cultured and infused back into the patient. Provenge, developed by Dendreon was the first cancer vaccine (dendritic cell based) approved in the U.S. Adoptive immunotherapies like CAR-T technology also falls under this category.

CAR-T technology:

CAR-T (chimeric antigen receptor expressing T cells) are bioengineered T cells that are modified to express a specific tumor receptor. Typically, these receptors are used to graft the specificity of a monoclonal antibody onto a T cell; with transfer of their coding sequence facilitated by retroviral vectors. CAR-modified T cells can be engineered to target virtually any tumor-associated antigen. Following the collection of a patient's T cells, the cells are genetically engineered to express CARs specifically directed towards antigens on the patient's tumor cells, then infused back into the patient (autologous technique). Side effects like cytokine response storm have been

seen in early clinical studies of this technology, which can poten-
tially be managed by introduction of a suicide gene. Early studies
using this technology have shown promising results, which will be
discussed in more detail later in the text under companies like Juno
Therapeutics and Kite Pharmaceuticals.

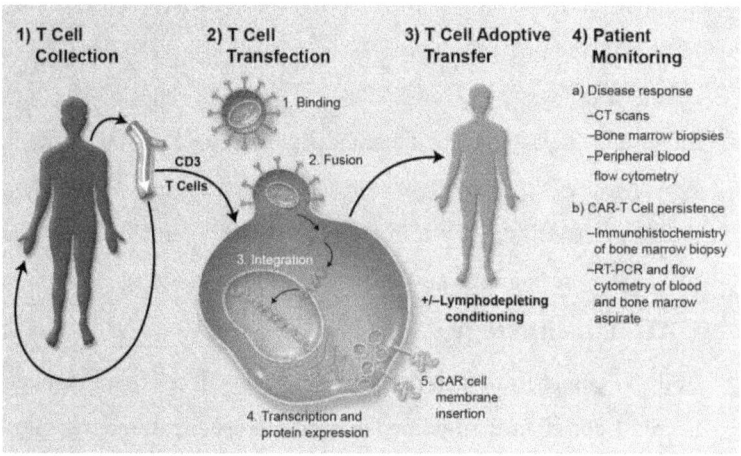

CAR-T technology[5]

Targeted cancer therapies:

Targeted cancer therapies are drugs that target specific molecular
targets or mutations, like Epidermal Growth Factor Receptor
(EGFR) mutation in lung cancer and BRAF mutation in melanoma.
Targeted therapies are an example of personalized medicine or pre-
cision medicine, which involves developing therapies that are indi-
vidualized to a patient. While not specifically considered cancer
immunotherapy, targeted therapies are either small molecules or

monoclonal antibodies (which may be considered cancer immuno-therapy). Small molecule compounds have targets that are located inside the cell since these drugs are able to penetrate the cell wall easily due to small size. Monoclonal antibodies have relatively large size and usually have targets that are outside cells or on the cell sur-face.

14

CHAPTER 4

Our Select List of Cancer Therapy Companies

My top picks for most promising companies developing revolutionary cancer treatments are discussed in this chapter. The list is by no way all-inclusive and I have focused on companies that I believe will provide the most risk-adjusted return to investors over next 3-5 years (ranging from minimum 50 to over 100 percent). Mostly, I have tried to include companies with a broad pipeline and multiple product candidates in development, which allows a 'margin of safety' and multiple shots at the target even if one of the product candidates fails in clinical trials. Partnerships or collaborations with larger biotechnology or biopharmaceutical players as well as significant ownership by large institutional owners like hedge funds also add more confidence in a company with products still under development. For an emerging biotechnology company, having adequate cash reserves to conduct clinical trials is also important. My selection checklist also included factors like insider transactions (insider buying adds confidence to an investment) and quality of management. Few other public companies, which investors may consider buying are mentioned in chapter 5.

The biotechnology sector pullback of summer 2015 has created even more attractive entry points for gems like Juno, Kite, Bluebird Bio and NanKwest. I believe that this pullback has provided investors with a significant buying opportunity, which will be rewarded over next 2-3 years.

The stock price targets mentioned in this chapter are estimated based on my own calculations and other research analysts. Investors are advised to do their own due diligence regarding these price targets.

Disclaimer:

The author and the firm, Vasuda Capital Management hold long positions in all the stocks mentioned in this chapter. I wrote this book myself, and it expresses my own opinions. I have no business relationship with any company whose stock is mentioned in this article. This is not an investment advice and investors are suggested to do their own research before investing.

Cancer Immunotherapy Companies, including CAR-T based therapies:

Juno Therapeutics (JUNO, NASDAQ)

Juno Therapeutics is one of the key companies in the CAR-T (chimeric antigen receptor T cells) and TCRs (T cell receptors) space in cancer therapeutics.

Juno's CAR-T technology (armored T-cell technology) uses mechanisms to either amplify or inhibit T cell activation signals present in the cancer cells or the tumor microenvironment. Juno's technology is a third generation CAR technology that incorporates a CD28 or 4-1BB co-stimulatory signaling domain to mimic a "second signal" that amplifies the activation of the CAR T cells, leading to a more robust signal to the T cell to multiply and kill the cancer cell.

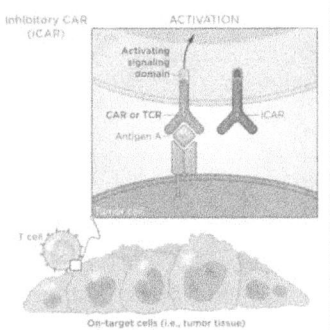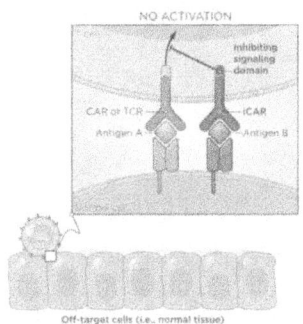

(Image adapted from the Company's website)

T-cell receptor (TCR) technology differs from CAR-T technology that TCRs can be engineered for targets both on the surface and inside T-cells (CARs only target antigens on the surface of tumor cells). TCR technology may allow devising T cells specific to a patient alone, thus allowing a highly personalized approach.

In early phase 1 studies in acute lymphocytic leukemia (ALL) using Juno's product JCAR015, a remarkable 91 percent complete response rate was seen. The study is expected to be completed in January 2016. In adult ALL using the product JCAR 014, even more impressive 100 percent complete response rate was seen.

The company won a vote of confidence from Celgene, the large biotechnology company who collaborated with Juno for developing CAR-T and T cell receptor (TCR) technologies. Under the terms of the agreement, Celgene made an initial payment of approximately $1 billion which includes the purchase of ~9.1 million shares of Juno stock at $93.00 per share, with potential to increase its stake over time to a maximum of 30 percent.

Pipeline:

TARGET	PRODUCT CANDIDATE	TRIAL NUMBER	TRIAL DESCRIPTION
CD19	JCAR015	NCT01044069	Precursor B Cell Acute Lymphoblastic Leukemia (B-ALL) Treated With Autologous T Cells Genetically Targeted to the B Cell Specific Antigen CD19
CD19	JCAR015	NCT01840566	A Phase I Trial of High Dose Therapy and Autologous Stem Cell Transplantation Followed by Infusion of Chimeric Antigen Receptor (CAR) Modified T-Cells Directed Against CD19+ B-Cells for Relapsed and Refractory Aggressive B Cell Non-Hodgkin Lymphoma
CD19	JCAR017	NCT02028455	A Pediatric and Young Adult Trial of Genetically Modified T Cells Directed Against CD19 for Relapsed/Refractory CD19+ Leukemia
CD19	JCAR014	NCT01865617	Laboratory Treated T Cells in Treating Patients With Relapsed or Refractory Chronic Lymphocytic Leukemia, Non-Hodgkin Lymphoma, or Acute Lymphoblastic Leukemia
WT-1	JTCR016	NCT01640301	Phase I/II Study of Adoptive Immunotherapy After Allogeneic HCT With Virus Specific CD8+ T Cells That Have Been Transduced to Express a WT1-Specific T Cell Receptor for Patients With High Risk or Relapsed AML, MDS, or CML
WT-1	JCTR016	NCT02408016	Phase I/II Study in WT1-Expressing Non-small Cell Lung Cancer and Mesothelioma, Comparing Cellular Adoptive Immunotherapy With Polyclonal Autologous Central Memory to Naïve CD8+ T Cells That Have Been Transduced to Express a WT1-Specific T Cell Receptor
CD22	JCAR018	NCT02315612	Phase I Dose Escalation Study of Anti-CD22 Chimeric Receptor T Cells In Pediatric and Young Adults With Recurrent or Refractory CD22-expressing B Cell Malignancies
L1-CAM	JCAR023	NCT02311621	A Phase 1 Feasibility and Safety Study of Cellular Immunotherapy for Recurrent/Refractory Neuroblastoma Using Autologous T-cells Lentivirally Transduced to Express CD171-specific Chimeric Antigen Receptors

(Image adapted from the Company's website)

In addition, Juno is developing a MUC-16/IL-12 product candidate in ovarian cancer, which is its first development candidate that uses the "armored" CAR technology.

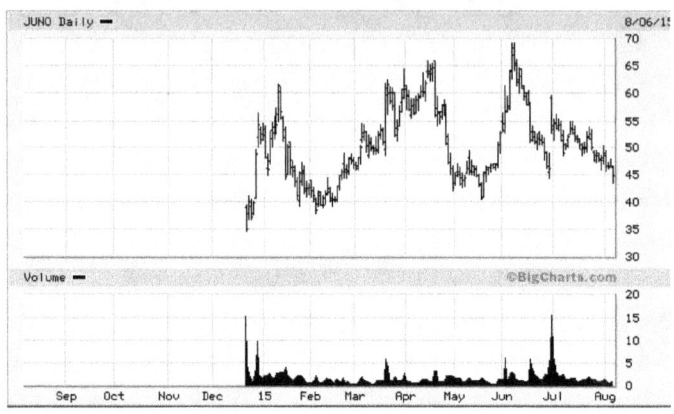

Stock Price target: $120

Financials: Cash in hand as of Q1, 2015: $ 395.59 million.

Partnerships: Research partnerships with Fred Hutchinson Cancer Research Center, Seattle, WA; Memorial Sloan Kettering Hospital, New York; Seattle Children's Research Institute, Seattle, WA.

The scientific advisors include prominent physicians from leading cancer centers like Memorial Sloan-Kettering, NY.

Risks of Investment:

Most of the above products are early clinical studies and will take many years before they are commercialized. Other competitors in the CAR-T space include Kite Pharmaceuticals and Cellectis. Other immunotherapies like Nankwest's NK cells are also a

20

potential threat to CAR-T and TCR technologies. Large-scale production of T cells when they have to be taken from a patient also raises questions.

Juno is our number-one pick in the CAR-T and TCR space and our investment philosophy is supported by Celgene's investment.

Kite Pharmaceuticals (KITE, NASDAQ)

Kite Pharmaceuticals is our second ranked pick in the CAR-T space after Juno. The company's collaborations include National Cancer Institute, Blue Bird Bio, Leukemia and Lymphoma Society and Amgen. Kite's scientific advisors include Professor Zelig Eshhar, one of the early developers of CARs in the 1980s. Kite's CAR-T cells are also autologous (taken from the patient) like Juno.

Pipeline:

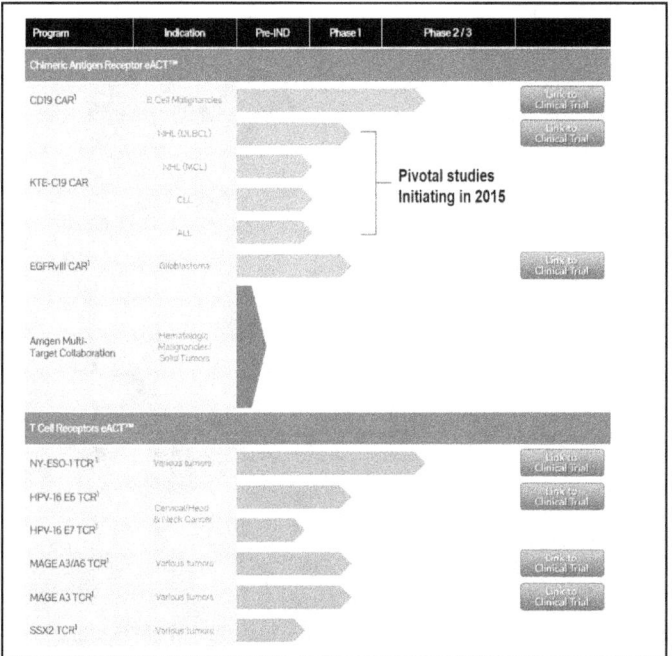

(Image adapted from the Company's website)

Kite's CD-19 CARs are in a more advanced phase 2/3 stage in B cell malignancies than Juno but Juno has shown higher tumor response rates so far in early studies. Early studies showed 76% objective response rate in Non-Hodgkin's lymphoma (NHL) and chronic lymphocytic leukemia (CLL). Early studies of both Juno and Kite have shown that side-effects like cytokine response syndrome are easily manageable with dose titration.

In addition, Kite is also doing a different immunotherapy called Dc-Ad CM-CAIX in clear cell type renal cell cancer.

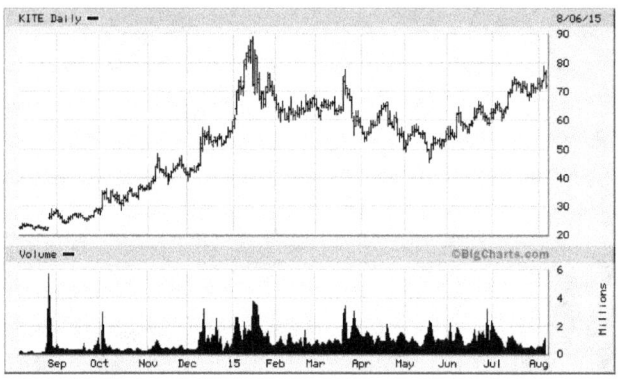

Stock Price target: $ 120

Financials: Cash Q1, 2015: $ 428.53 million.

Risks of investment: Like Juno, the products are in early stages and there is no guarantee of success in later stage clinical trials. There is also threat from technologies like Nankwest's NK cells.

Cellectis, A,D,R, (CLLS, NASDAQ)

Cellectis uses <u>allogeneic</u> CAR-T immunotherapy rather than the autologous approach used by Juno and Kite. T cells are isolated from healthy individuals (rather than the patient) and then modified to attack tumor cells. Allogeneic T cells engineered by Cellectis may be used to overcome the limitations of autologous CAR-T immunotherapy.

Pipeline

Product name Targeted indication	Discovery	CAR T-cell engineering	In Vitro Studies	In Vivo Studies	CTA/IND* filing	Alliance
UCART19 Acute Lymphoblastic Leukemia (ALL) Chronic Lymphocytic Leukemia (CLL)					2015	Servier
UCART123 Acute Myeloid Leukemia (AML)						Wholly-Owned
UCART38 Multiple Myeloma (MM)				Q4 2015		Wholly-Owned
UCARTCS1 Multiple Myeloma (MM)				Q4 2015		Wholly-Owned

(Image adapted from Cellectis website)

There was an impressive 92 percent objective response rate in early clinical studies using UCART-91 in ALL and CLL including complete remission in 8 patients. Phase 1 trials are expected to start in 2016.

Partnerships:

25

Cellectis has partnerships with Servier for UCART-19 in B cell malignancies and 5 other candidates in solid tumors. It also has partnership with Pfizer for drug development in 15 tumor targets.

Stock Price target: $ 54

Management: The founder-CEO, Andre Choulika is a pioneer in nuclease-based gene editing.

Financials: Cash/cash equivalents of $135 million as of Q4, 2014.

Bellicum Pharmaceuticals (BLCM, NASDAQ)

Bellicum Pharmaceuticals' focus is in discovering immune therapies for various hematological cancers and solid tumors and orphan inherited blood disorders.

The company's lead product candidate BPX-501 is an adjunct T-cell therapy administered after allogeneic hematopoietic stem cell transplantation. The company's next lead product candidate, BPX-201 is a dendritic cell cancer vaccine being evaluated in metastatic castrate-resistant prostate cancer. In addition, several CAR-T and TCR therapies are being evaluated in hematological cancers and solid tumors.

Pipeline:

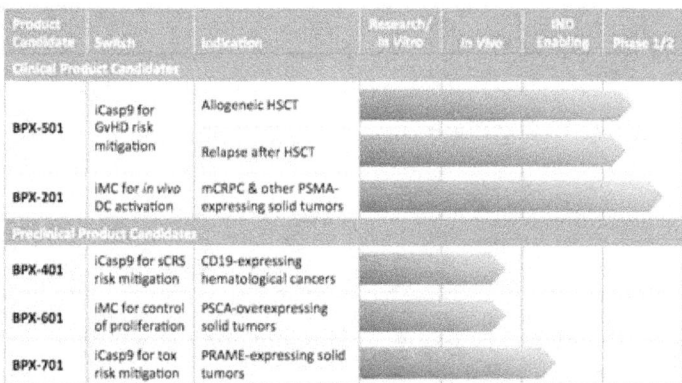

(Image adapted from Bellicum Pharmaceuticals website)

The key feature of Bellicum's technology is the use switch technologies to control cytokine release syndrome, CRS (a potential side effect in CAR based therapies). At the earliest signs of CRS, a drug is infused which eliminates the T cells. There is a potential of incorporating these switch technologies with CARs being developed by other companies like Juno and Kite. Also, there are currently no products targeting prostate stem cell antigen (PSCA, being targeted by BPX-601), which may be expressed in solid tumors like prostate, pancreatic, bladder, esophageal and gastric cancers.

A table demonstrating various switch technologies being developed by Bellicum is given below (adapted from Bellicum's website).

	CaspaCIDe	CIDeCAR	GoCAR-T	DeCIDe
Cell Type	Donor T cells (HSCT) or patient T cells (CAR-T or TCRs)	Patient T cells	Patient T cells	Patient dendritic cells
Proprietary Component	caspase-9 switch	caspase-9 switch + MC	MC switch	MC switch
Applications	HSCT TCR Therapy	CAR-T Therapy	CAR-T Therapy	Cancer Vaccine
Potential Safety Benefit	Can modulate effect with rimiducid which triggers T-cell apoptosis	Can modulate effect with rimiducid which triggers T-cell apoptosis	Can modulate effect with rimiducid which triggers T-cell activation & proliferation	Limited life span and do not proliferate
Potential Efficacy Benefit	Widens therapeutic window for maximum benefit from treatment	Widens therapeutic window; MC may enhance T-cell potency	Widens therapeutic window; MC may enhance T-cell potency	May help avoid inhibitory effects of the immune system
Product Candidates	BPX-501 BPX-701	BPX-401	BPX-601	BPX-201

28

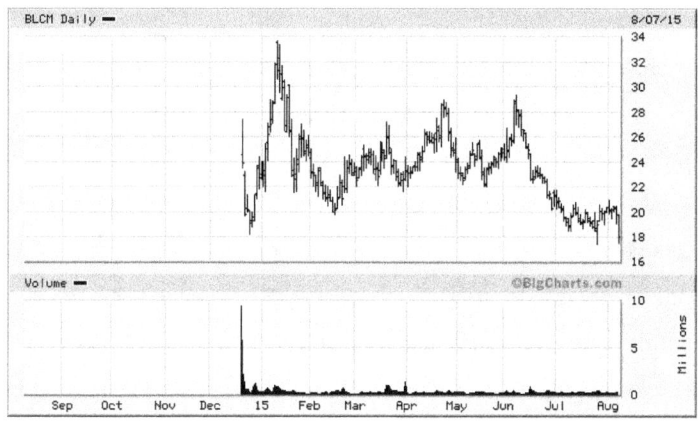

Stock Price target: $ 40.

Collaborations: National Cancer Institute is collaborating with Bellicum on clinical trials in sarcoma and other solid tumors based on its proprietary switch technology.

Financials: $ 183.64 million (03/15).

Near-term catalysts: Phase 1 / 2 data of BPX-501 in hematological stem cell transplant is expected in second half of 2015.

Notably, large healthcare based hedge funds like Baker Brothers (15.9% of outstanding shares) and RA Capital (3.9% of outstanding shares) hold significant stakes in Bellicum Pharmaceuticals.

Ziopharm Oncology (ZIOP, NASDAQ)

Ziopharm is another biotechnology company in the cell-based therapies for cancer. The company's stock price has been in a strong uptrend over past few months since announcing a collaboration with MD Anderson Cancer Center for its CAR-T and other cell-based therapies. The company also has a collaboration with Intrexon Corporation for using Intrexon's proprietary Rheoswitch technology to control gene expression and control side-effects like cytokine release syndrome. Rheoswitch is the only biological switch tested in humans so far. Unlike lentiviral/retroviral approach of CARs (Juno, Kite), Ziopharm's technology is non-viral based.

There was also a buyout rumor for Ziopharm in June 2015. A prominent analyst estimated an expected buyout price of $ 5-10 billion in the next 18 months, which is a significant upside from the current stock price.

Pipeline:

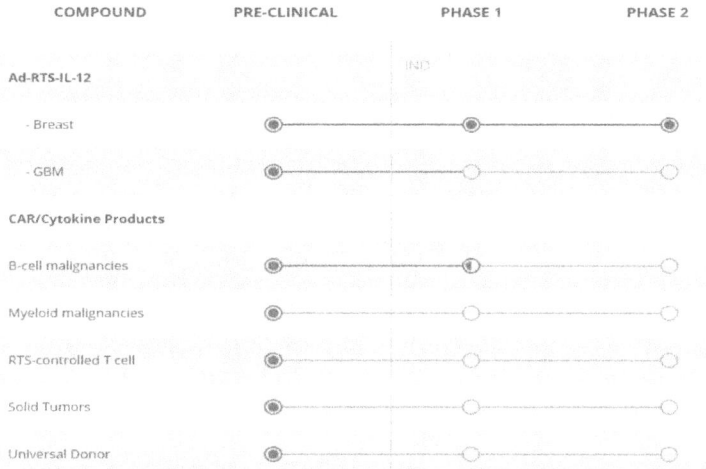

COMPOUND	PRE-CLINICAL	PHASE 1	PHASE 2

Ad-RTS-IL-12

- Breast

- GBM

CAR/Cytokine Products

B-cell malignancies

Myeloid malignancies

RTS-controlled T cell

Solid Tumors

Universal Donor

(Image adapted from Ziopharm's website)

Most of the product candidates are still in early studies as shown in the pipeline given below. Phase 1 results of Ad-RTS-IL-12 in malignant glioma are expected in December 2016.

Rheoswitch therapeutic System:

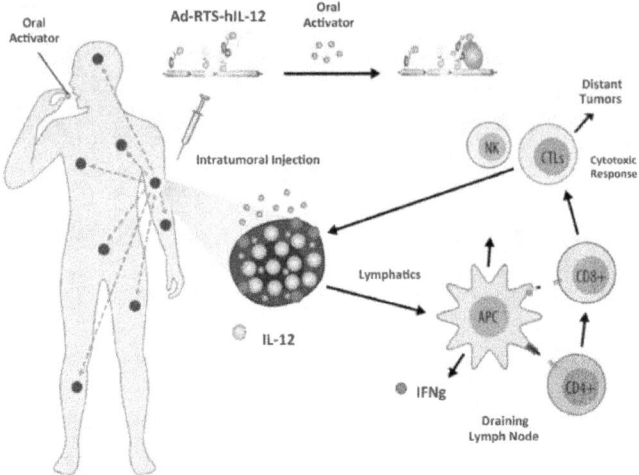

(Image adapted from Ziopharm's website)

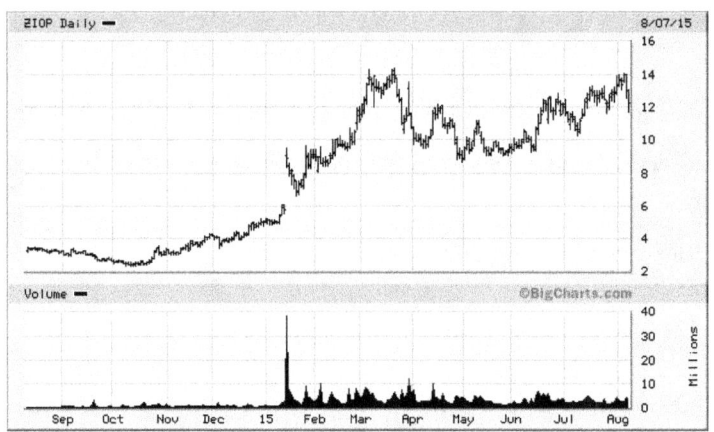

Price target: $ 20.

Management: The CEO, Laurence Copper is a professor at MD Anderson Cancer Center and is a pioneer in CARs.

Financials: Cash: $ 129.68 million, enough to last about 2 years.

Partnerships: MD Anderson Cancer Center and Intrexon Corporation.

Insider transactions: Kirk Randall, the CEO of Intrexon bought 1.44 Million shares of Ziopharm at $ 18.75 each in February 2015. He again bought 8,222,953 shares on 6/4/2015. Kirk Randall's venture capital firm, Third Security, LLC owns 15 percent of Ziopharm's outstanding shares.

The prominent hedge fund, Orbimed Advisors owns 1.98 percent of Ziopharm's outstanding shares. Texas University Investment Management Company owns 9.14 percent of outstanding shares. This demonstrates significant confidence in Ziopharm's product candidates.

Sorrento Therapeutics (SRNE, NASDAQ)

Sorrento's product pipeline highlight is CAR-natural killer cells against various types of cancers. The company has partnership with Dr. Patrick So--Shiong (of NantKwest and the inventor of Abraxane) to develop cancer immunotherapies. Unlike, most CAR-T cell based therapies, CAR-NK cell based therapies are not autologous and have the potential for large scale production. In early studies, no cytokine release syndrome has been seen unlike CAR-T cell based therapies.

Sorrento's products are still in very early clinical stages. Initiation of phase-1 studies for CAR-TNK cells is expected in 2016.

Pipeline:

(Image adapted from Sorrento's website)

The company formed a subsidiary called TNK Therapeutics (in partnership with NantKwest) in May 2014, which will focus on developing CAR-NK cell based therapies in various hematological cancers and solid tumors. In addition, the pipeline also includes antibody-drug conjugates and small molecule targeted therapies in cancer.

Resiniferatoxin (RTX) is a novel non-opiate analgesic which is given intrathecal or epi-thecal route and has been shown to reduce opioid utilization in case-studies. Phase-2 trials are expected to begin in 2016.

Sorrento also has partnership with Advaxis for immuno-oncology therapies.

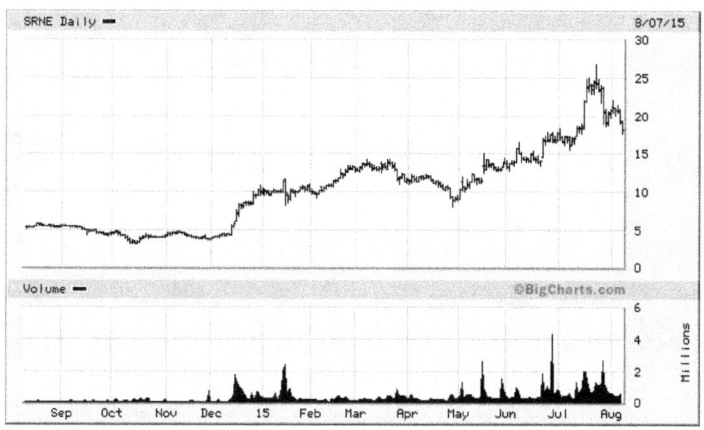

Stock Price target: $ 30

Financials: Cash $ 60.5 Millions.

35

Dr. Patrick Shoo-Shiong owns about 8 million shares of Sorrento.

Sorrento's management is excellent at acquiring molecules from other companies and then developing and selling them at higher price. For example, Cynviloq, next generation Paclitaxel was acquired by Sorrento for $ 27.8 million and sold for $ 2.9 billion to Nantpharm in March, 2015.

Nankwest (NK, NASDAQ)

The company is owned by Dr. Patrick Soon-Shiong, the billionaire physician-scientist and the inventor of the blockbuster cancer drug, Abraxane. The company launched its IPO in July, 2015 with a small float of 7.8 percent.

Technology: The company's platform uses natural killer (NK) cells rather than the T-cells being utilized by other CAR-T companies like Juno.

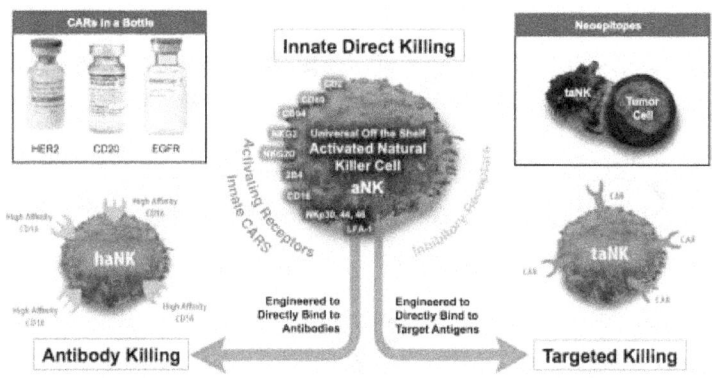

(Images adapted from the Nankwest website.)

Mechanism of action of activated NK cells.

STAGE 1	STAGE 2	STAGE 3
Binding of Receptors	**Activation of Granzymes**	**Release of Granzymes**
Adhesion	Activation	Apoptosis
Synapse Connection	Perforin & Granzyme Delivery	Cell Death

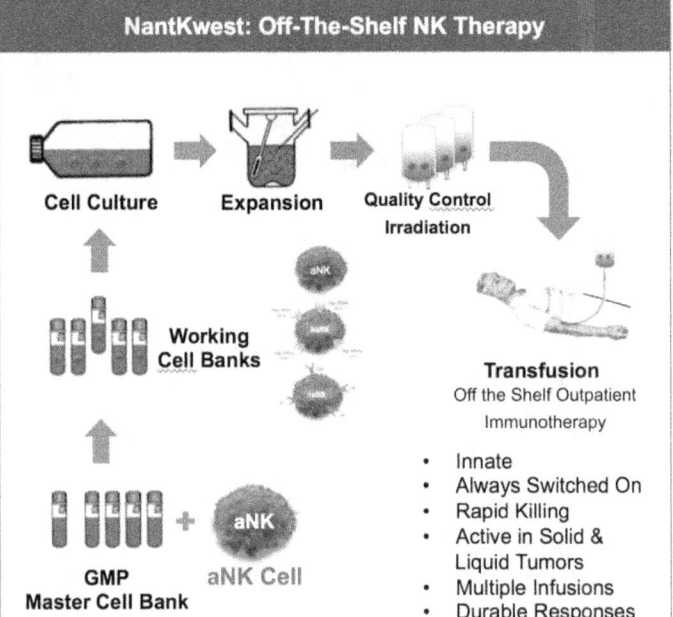

Nankwest's proprietary NK cell technology can also be modified to express CARs (chimeric antigen receptors) which can be targeted to specific cancer cells. The advantages over CAR-T cell technology (Juno, Kite etc.) is that the NK cells do not need to be autologous (taken from the patient, though Cellectis has allogenic CAR-T technology). This theoretically allows larger scale production of immune cells.

The first clinical trials of NK's technology are expected to launch in 2016. The most advanced NK cell line expresses a CAR for ErbB2 (also known as Her2), a protein commonly found on breast, ovary, gastric, bladder and medulloblastoma (brain) cancers. This strategy has multiple advantages over other CAR approaches using patient or donor sourced effector cells such as autologous T-cells, especially in terms of scalability, quality control and consistency.

Leadership: The Chairman, Dr. Soon-Shiong, a physician, surgeon and scientist, has pioneered novel therapies for both diabetes and cancer, published over 100 scientific papers, and has over 95 issued patents on groundbreaking advancements spanning myriad fields. Dr. Soon-Shiong performed the world's first encapsulated human islet transplant, the first engineered islet cell transplant and the first pig to man islet cell transplant in diabetic patients. He invented and developed Abraxane, the nation's first FDA-approved protein nano-particle albumin-bound delivery technology for the treatment of cancer.

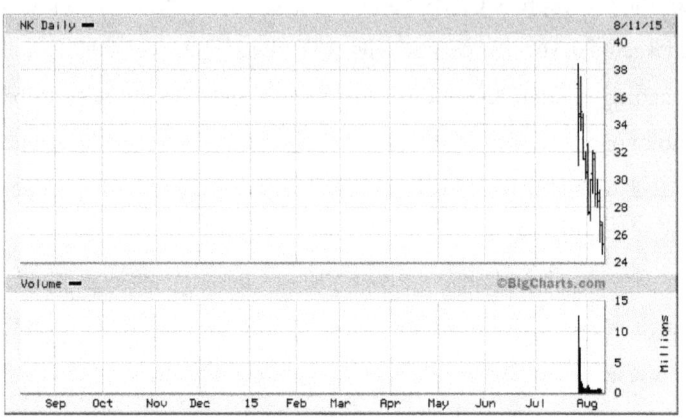

Stock Price Target: $ 45

Financials: Cash of $ 49.85 million as of Q2, 2015.

Blue Bird Bio (BLUE, NASDAQ)

Blue Bird Bio is well-known for its promising gene therapy results in early clinical studies in rare diseases like childhood cerebral adrenoleukodystrophy (CCALD) and hematological diseases like sickle cell disease and thalassemia. The company also has an impressive immuno-oncology program using the CAR-T technology, targeting B-cell maturation antigen (BCMA, a cell surface protein that is expressed in normal plasma cells and in most multiple myeloma cells) and the human papillomavirus type 16 E6 (HPV-16 E6). The company has partnerships with First Prime Therapeutics testing T cell and gene therapies in hematologic malignancies and solid tumors. It has also partnered with Kite Pharmaceuticals to develop second generation TCR product candidates directed against HPV-16 E6. It also collaborated with Celgene and Baylor College of Medicine to develop CAR T cell therapies with its initial focus on BCMA. The phase 1 clinical trial testing BCMA as a target is expected to start in early 2016. In addition, the company is also exploring gene editing, which is considered the next frontier in gene therapy.

Pipeline:

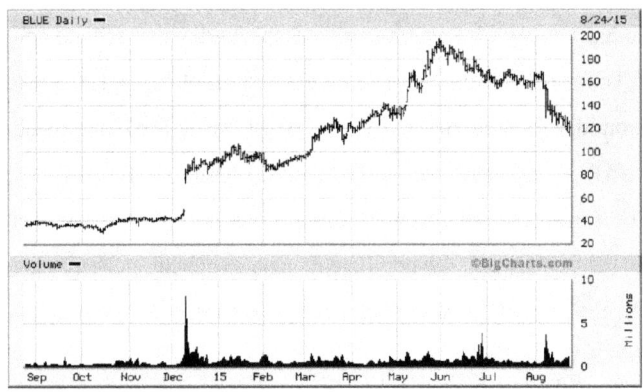

Product Candidates	Program Area	Preclinical	Phase 1/2	Phase 2/3	Rights/Partner
Lenti-D™	CNS Diseases				Worldwide
LentiGlobin	Rare Hemaglobinopathies				Worldwide
	Severe Sickle Cell Disease				Worldwide
bb2121 BCMA	Oncology				Celgene
Next Gen BCMA	Multiple Myeloma				Celgene
Five Prime Target					Worldwide
Other Programs					Worldwide
Early Pipeline	Research				Worldwide

* The current clinical trials for LentiGlobin are Phase 1/2 studies that may provide the basis for early conditional approval in some jurisdictions.

(Image adapted from the company website, investor presentation.)

Stock Price Target: $220

Financials: Cash of $810.51 Million, Q1, 2015.

The company stock is widely held by institutional investors like Capital Research Global Investors (12.08% of the float) and Baillie Gifford and Company (10.2% of the float).

First Prime Therapeutics (FPRX, NASDAQ)

First Prime Therapeutics has a broad pipeline. FPA008 is a CSF1R antibody being tested in 6 cancers in combination with Bristol Myers' check-point inhibitor, Nivolumab. The molecule is also being tested in pigmented vilonodular sinusitis (PVNS) with phase 1 initial data expected in late 2015 to early 2016. Phase 1 data of FPA144 in gastric cancer is expected in end of 2016. Preliminary data of FP-1039 in squamous non-small cell lung cancer and mesothelioma is also expected in end 2015. Besides FPA008, the company also has an impressive immuno-oncology program in GITR antibodies and CAR-T cell technology (licensed to BluBird).

Pipeline:

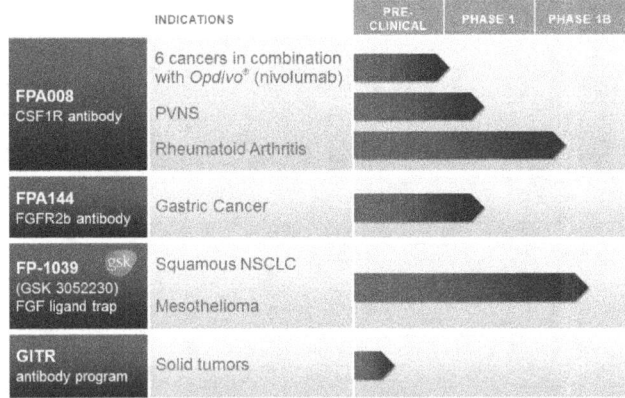

(Image adapted from the company website)

Partnerships/ collaborations with key companies:

44

	PRODUCT	INITIATED
bluebirdbio	CAR T Cell License Agreement	May 2015
Bristol-Myers Squibb	FPA008 Immuno-Oncology Clinical Collaboration	November 2014
HUMAN GENOME SCIENCES	FP-1039 (GSK 3052230) FGF Ligand Trap License Agreement	March 2011
	RESEARCH AREA	INITIATED
Bristol-Myers Squibb	Immuno-Oncology	March 2014
ucb	Fibrosis and CNS	March 2013
gsk	Respiratory Diseases	April 2012

(Image adapted from the company website).

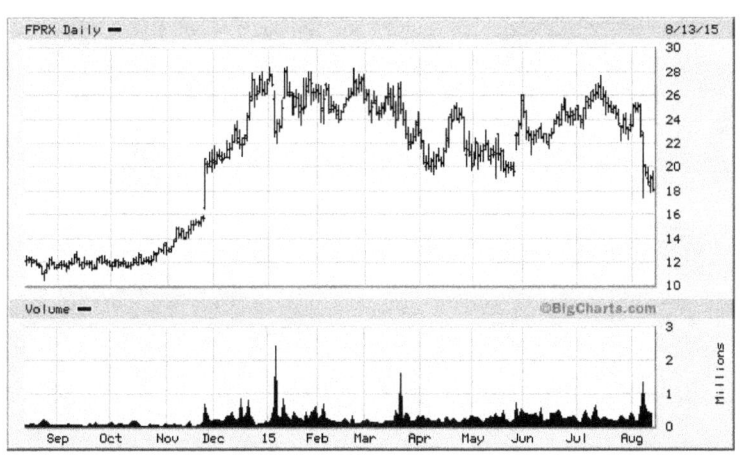

The stock price has retreated from its 52 week high of $ 28 and is offering an attractive buying point.

Stock Price target: $35. Oppenheimer has a price target of $ 45.

Adage Capital Partners, the well-known hedge fund owns 6.25% of the stock float as of Q1, 2015.

Lion Biotechnologies (LBIO, NASDAQ)

The company's lead product is focused on cancer immunotherapy using infiltrating T cells (TILs). Notably, these T cells are not tumor antigen targeted like Juno or Kite. In phase 2 clinical trials in metastatic malignant melanoma, patients treated with the therapy showed objective response rates of 49 percent vs. 32% objective response rate in Bristol Myers Opdivo trial. The therapy also has potential applications in ovarian, colorectal, head and neck and other cancers. There is a potential of combining the therapy with checkpoint inhibitors.

Pipeline:

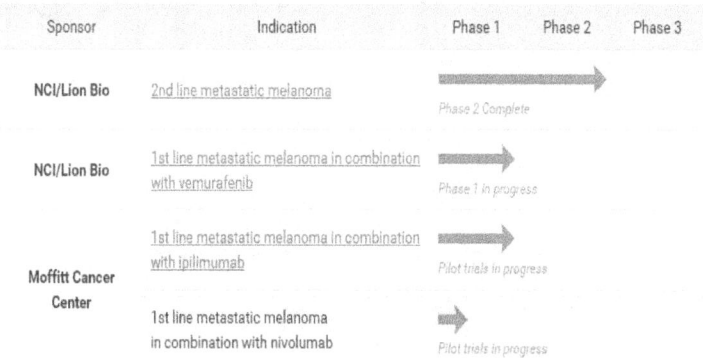

(Image adapted from the company website)

LN-144 has an orphan-drug designation in malignant melanoma and the phase 2 trial is expected to be completed in September 2019.

Partnerships: National Cancer Institute (adoptive immunotherapies for malignant melanoma), Moffitt Cancer Center.

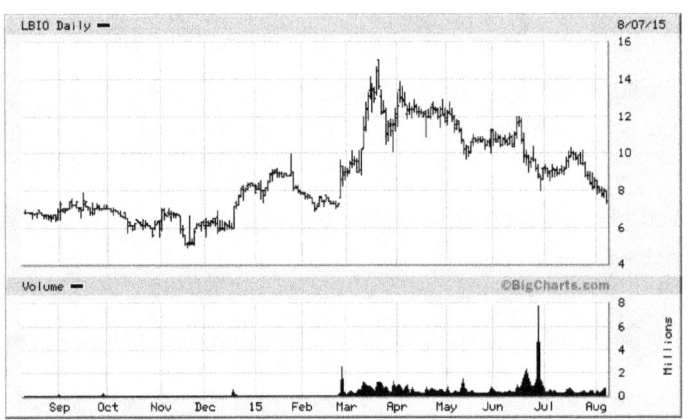

Stock Price target: $20

Financials: Cash of $ 11.28 Millions, Q1 2015.

The company's management team is excellent; for example the Chief Scientific Officer, has about 25 years of research experience in tumor-infiltrating lymphocytes.

The notable hedge fund, Baker Brothers own 2.94 percent of outstanding shares as of Q1, 2014.

Calithera Biosciences (CALA, NASDAQ)

Calithera Biosciences is involved in developing small molecule based therapies in various cancers as well as immuno-oncology. Calithera's lead product candidate, CB-839 is a first-in the class glutaminase inhibitor in three phase 1 trials. The drug blocks the ability of tumor cells to use glutamine to grow and survive. The drug has shown broad antitumor activity across 122 tumor cell lines including cancers of the breast, kidney, lung, mesothelioma, lymphoma, and multiple myeloma in preclinical studies. CB-839 is also synergistic with signaling pathway inhibitors showing potential to combined with various drugs for renal cell cancer, non-small cell lung cancer, sarcoma and melanoma. In addition, Calithera's lead preclinical program in tumor immunology is directed at developing inhibitors of the enzyme arginase and may provide a first-in-class therapeutic agent for this novel target.

Pipeline:

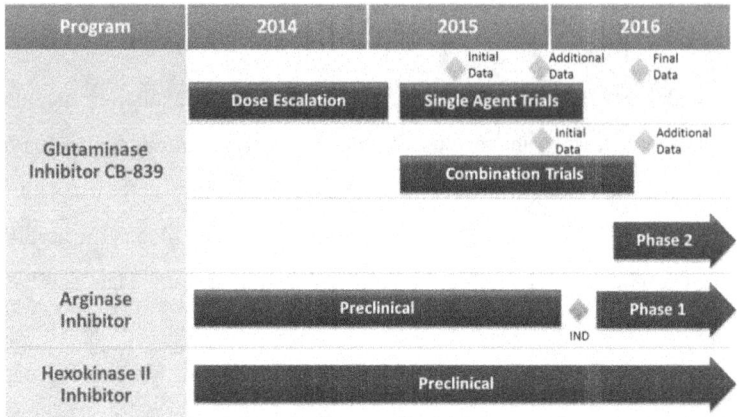

(Image adopted from Calithera's website)

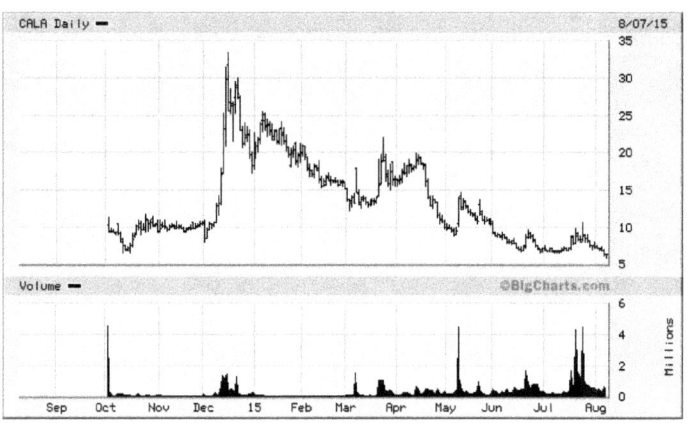

Stock price target: $20

Financials: The Company has cash of $ 94 million in Q1, 2015.

Adage Capital Partners, which was founded by former money managers at Harvard University Endowment Management, owns 15.4% of outstanding shares of Calithera Biosciences at $7-8 per share since Q4 2014.

Advaxis Immunotherapies (ADXS, NASDAQ)

Advaxis is a clinical stage cancer immunotherapy company which has created or is developing more than 20 immunotherapies based on its proprietary *Lm* technology. The technology involves infusing live attenuated Gram positive bacteria (Listeria Monocytogenes) that tricks body's immune system into thinking that cancer cells are infected by these bacteria and should be eliminated.

Pipeline:

INDICATION	PHASE 1	PHASE 2	PHASE 3	TRIALS
ADXS-HPV				
CERVICAL* AIM2CERV				
CERVICAL* METASTATIC CERVICAL		Phase 2		
CERVICAL* METASTATIC - GOG		Phase 2		View Trial
CERVICAL* COMBO WITH MEDI 4736¹	Phase 1/2			View Trial
CERVICAL* METASTATIC SINGLE ARM HIGH DOSE	Phase 1/2			View Trial
HEAD AND NECK* NEOADJUVANT WINDOW OF OPPORTUNITY - MOUNT SINAI		Phase 2		View Trial
HEAD & NECK* METASTATIC - COMBO WITH MEDI 4736¹	Phase 1/2			View Trial
ANAL* ADJUVANT SINGLE ARM IN HIGH RISK - BROWN UNIVERSITY		Phase 2		View Trial
ANAL* METASTATIC		Phase 2		
ADXS-PSA				
PROSTATE COMBO WITH KEYTRUDA®²	Phase 1/2			View Trial
ADXS-HER2				
HER2 OVEREXPRESSING TUMORS (IND APPROVED)	Phase 1			

Completed   In Progress   Planned

(Image adopted from the company website)

ADXS-HPV: The product candidate is in phase 2 clinical trials in recurrent cervical cancer with an estimated completion date of June 2017. The molecule was tested in a successful phase 2 trial in India in this population.

The molecule is also being tested in an ongoing phase 1 / 2 clinical trial in HPV-associated Head and Neck cancers and phase 1 / 2 clinical trial in anal cancer. In preliminary analysis of ADXS-HPV in anal cancer, there was an impressive 100 percent response rate.

ADXS-PSA: It is being tested in an ongoing phase 1 / 2 trial in previously treated metastatic castration resistant prostate cancer.

ADXS-HER2: Ongoing phase 1 trial in osteosarcoma (orphan drug designation), also in cancers of breast, gastric and esophageal tumors.

Partnerships: Medimmune, Merck, Incyte (combining IDO inhibitor with ADXS-HPV in HPV associated cervical cancer). Sorrento therapeutics (combining immunotherapies with Sorrento's checkpoint inhibitors).

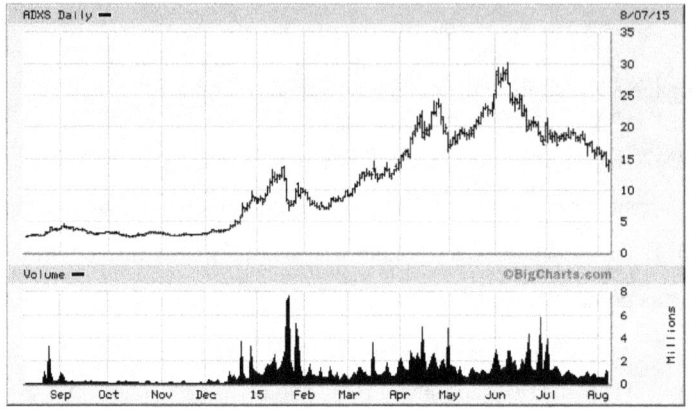

The stock price had a huge run from $3 in November 2014 to a high of $ 30 but has corrected and is providing an attractive entry point at present.

Stock Price Target: $ 30

Financials: Cash of $ 45.94 million as of Q1, 2015.

The prominent hedge fund, Adage Capital Management, founded by money managers who were earlier at Harvard University's endowment, bought about 500,000 shares at $19 per share in April, 2015 and hold about 16.3 percent of outstanding shares.

The company's competitor is Inovio, which is also developing cancer vaccines in cervical cancer.

Inovio Pharmaceuticals (INO, NASDAQ)

Inovio Pharmaceuticals technology is focused on cancer vaccines (next generation DNA-based vaccines), especially in human papilloma virus (HPV) based cancers. The company's therapies are being tested as a single agent and in combination with other cancer immunotherapies like check-point inhibitors.

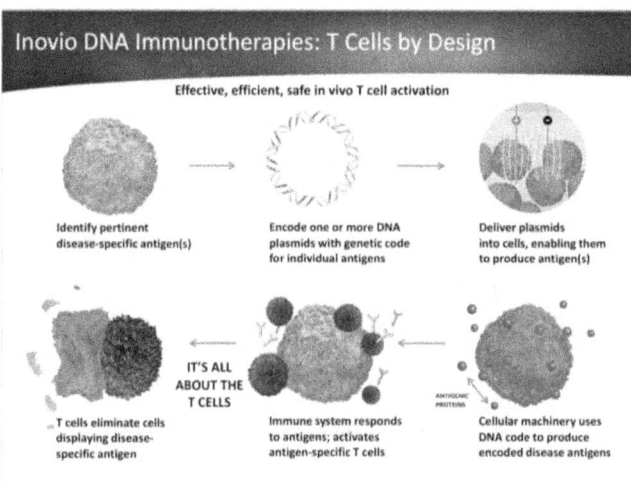

(Image adapted from the company website, investor presentation)

Immuno-oncology pipeline:

Product Name	Indication	Preclinical	Phase I	Phase II	Phase III
VGX-3100	CERVICAL DYSPLASIA				
INO-3112	CERVICAL CANCER			MedImmune	
INO-3112	HEAD & NECK CANCER			MedImmune	
INO-3106	AERODIGESTIVE CANCER				
INO-1400	BREAST/LUNG/PANCREATIC CANCERS				
INO-5150	PROSTATE CANCER				

(Image adapted from the company website)

Partnerships: Inovio has partnered with Medimmune, the specialty arm of Astra Zeneca, to test INO-312 with Medimmune's check point inhibitors in cervical cancer and head and neck cancer.

Inovio retains the rights to VGX-3100 which met its study end-points in a phase 2 clinical trial in cervical precancer. In this study, there was also clearance of HPV virus, raising the possibility of use as antiviral therapy in diseases like hepatitis B and HIV. The larger phase 3 trial is expected to begin in early 2016. Inovio retains the rights to HPV-associated precancers while HPV-associated cancers are licensed to MedImmune.

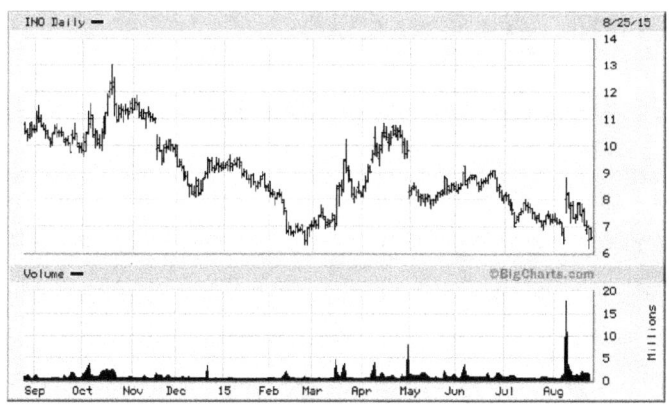

Stock Price target: $ 20

Financials: Cash of $154.6 million, Q2, 2015.

The company's scientific advisors include Dr. David Weiner, recognized as the "father of DNA vaccines," and other senior scientists, such as the developer of the rubella vaccine.

SPDR Biotech ETF (XBI) owns 4.6% of the stock float.

Agenus Bio (AGEN, NASDAQ)

Agenus Bio's key immuno-oncology technology is based on heat-shock protein (hsp-90) derived from the patient's own tumor to make a tumor-specific Prophage vaccine. In phase 2 data in glioblastoma multiforme (GBM), the vaccine has shown improved progression-free and overall survival. There was a better response in GBM patients with higher PDL-1 expression raising the potential of combining prophage vaccine with check-point inhibitors. In addition, the company has various checkpoint modulating antibodies and is collaborating with Incyte for some of these.

Agenus also had successful results in phase 3 trials in malaria and shingles vaccines (Glaxosmithkline partnership). The shingles vaccine being developed by Agenus can be used in immunocompromised patients and pregnancy unlike Mercks' vaccine.

Pipeline:

PLATFORM	DISEASE/TARGET	PARTNER(S)	PRECLINICAL	PH1	PH2	PH3	ANTICIPATED MILESTONES	
QS-21 Stimulon* Adjuvant	Malaria	GSK					BLA filed	✓
	Melanoma	GSK					Final Ph 3 data	2015
	Shingles	GSK					Ph 3 data	✓
	Alzheimer's disease	Pfizer/Janssen					Ph 2 data	2015+
	11 undisclosed programs	Partnered					Clinical data	2015+
Heat Shock Protein Vaccines	Glioma** (recurrent)						NCI study readout	Enrolling
	Glioma** (newly diagnosed)						Ph 2 data	✓
	Genital herpes (HerpV)						Ph 2 booster data	✓
	Melanoma + ipilimumab + CTX						Trial initiation	2015
Checkpoint Antibodies	GITR (agonist)	Incyte***						
	OX40 (agonist)	Incyte***						
	CTLA-4 (antagonist)						IND filings 2015/2016	
	PD-1 (antagonist)							
	TIM-3 (antagonist)	Incyte***						
	LAG-3 (antagonist)	Incyte***						
	Undisclosed	Merck					Undisclosed	
	Undisclosed	Merck					Undisclosed	

* Agenus is entitled to receive milestone payments and royalties from corporate partners upon successful achievement of milestone events and commercial sales, respectively.
** Globias/sole multiforme
*** Limited to hematology/oncology

Partnerships: Merck, Glaxosmithkline, Incyte.

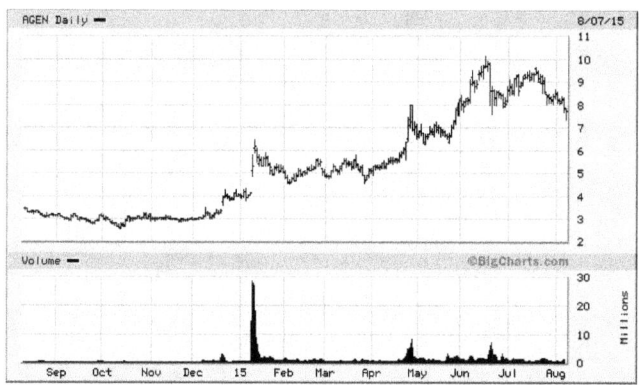

Price target: $ 25

Financials: Cash of $ 79 million, 03/2015.

Dynavax Technologies (DVAX, NASDAQ)

Dynavax's science involves developing product candidates which activate Toll-like receptors (TLRs) which are used by cells to recognize and respond to invading pathogens. By activating specific TLRs, the adaptive immune response can be enhanced, thus increasing the anticancer activity of drugs, for example in combination with check-point inhibitors. In contrast, inhibition of TLR signaling can be useful in many inflammatory and autoimmune diseases.

Pipeline:

Clinical Programs	Phase			
HEPLISAV-B Hepatitis B Vaccine	Pre-Clinical	Phase 1	Phase 2	Phase 3
SD-101 Cancer Immunotherapy	Pre-Clinical	Phase 1/2		
AZD1419 Asthma	Pre-Clinical	Phase 1	AstraZeneca	
DV1179 TLR 7/9 Inhibitor	Pre-Clinical	Phase 1		
DV230-NANOPARTICLE 2nd Generation Adjuvant	Pre-Clinical			

(Image adapted from the company's website)

60

The highlight of Dynavax's pipeline is SD-101 which showed significant anti-tumor activity in preclinical models. Intra-tumoral injection of SD-101 greatly increases CD8+ (killer) T cell infiltration into tumors. resulting in tumor volume reduction and improved survival in preclinical studies. The drug is also being studied in combination with checkpoint inhibitors (Merck collaboration). The ongoing phase 1 / 2 study in untreated low grade B cell lymphoma in combination with low dose radiation is estimated to finish in April, 2016. Another phase 1 study in combination with anti-PD1 inhibitor is being planned in metastatic melanoma. More studies are being planned in B cell lymphoma.

Dynavax's hepatitis B vaccine provides higher level of protection in just one month compared with current six month regime. The vaccine met its study end-points in a phase 3 study and is being investigated in a larger phase 3 trial.

AZD1419 is being investigated in atopic asthma in collaboration with AstraZeneca and phase 2 trial is being planned.

DV1179 is a toll cell receptor inhibitor being studied in autoimmune pancreatitis, scleroderma, dermatomyositis etc.

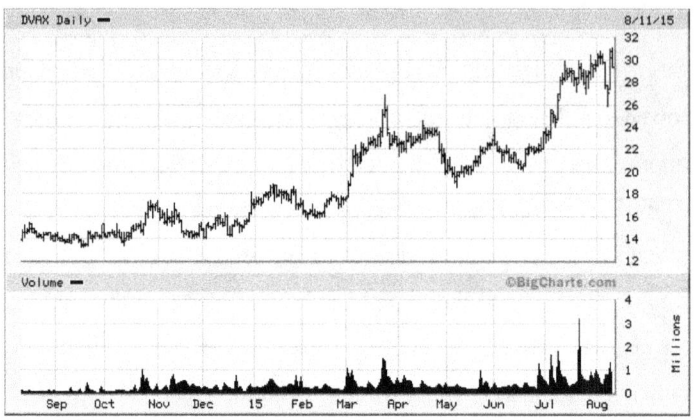

Stock Price Target: $ 42

Financials: Cash of $ 97.6 Millions as of Q1, 2015.

Dynavax's management team consists of prominent scientists like Robert Coffman, the Senior Vice President/Chief Scientific Officer and a pioneer in development of TLR agonists.

RA Capital, a prominent Boston-based hedge fund owns 8.87% of outstanding shares of Dynavax.

Oncomed (OMED, NASDAQ)

OncoMed Pharmaceuticals is focused on discovering and developing first-in-class monoclonal antibody therapeutics targeting cancer stem cells. Cancer stem cells are characterized by the ability to divide and give rise to new cancer stem cells and to change into the other cells that form the bulk of the tumor. Common cancer drugs target bulk tumor cells but have limited impact on cancer stem cells, thereby providing a path for cancer recurrence and metastases. Cancer stem cells have been discovered in various cancers like leukemia and solid tumors like cancers of the breast, lung, colon etc. Cancer stem cells appear to be resistant to both standard chemotherapy and radiation therapy. The company has advanced six novel anti-cancer stem cell product candidates into more than a dozen clinical studies.

Pipeline:

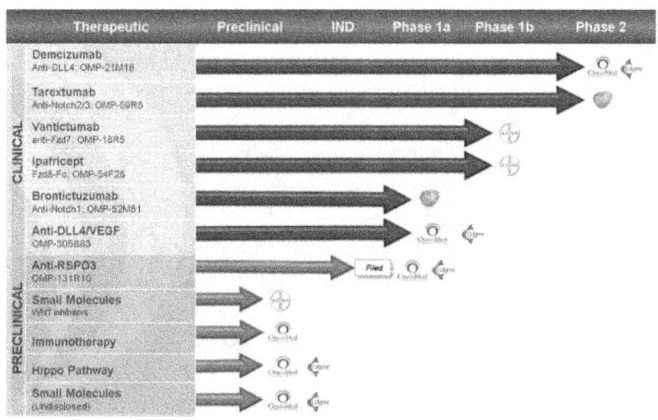

63

(Image adapted from the Company's website)

Four of these product candidates target the Notch cancer stem cell pathway, 2 products target Wnt cancer stem cell pathway and one product targets RSPO-LGR pathway. OMP-59R5 has been designated an orphan drug for the treatment of pancreatic cancer and small cell lung cancer. Other companies in the cancer stem cell space include Verastem, Geron, Immunocellular Therapeutics and Kalabios Therapeutics.

OMP-21M18, Demcizumab is being tested in ongoing phase 2 trials in non-small cell lung cancer and pancreatic cancer (estimated completion date of December 2015). It is also being tested in a phase 1b/2 trial in platinum-resistant ovarian cancer. OMP-59R5, Tarcxtumab is being tested in an ongoing phase 2 trial in advanced pancreatic cancer (GSK collaboration) with an estimated completion date of September 2016. OMP-54F28, Iprafricept is being tested in ongoing phase 1b trials in pancreatic cancer, hepatocellular cancer and ovarian cancer (Bayer collaboration). OMP-305B83 is anti-DLL4/VEGF in ongoing phase 1a study in refractory solid tumors (Celgene collaboration). OMP-131R10 is a first-in-class antibody being tested in collaboration with Celgene. In addition, various T cell activating agents are at preclinical stage of studies.

Partnerships: GlaxoSmithKline, Bayer, Celgene.

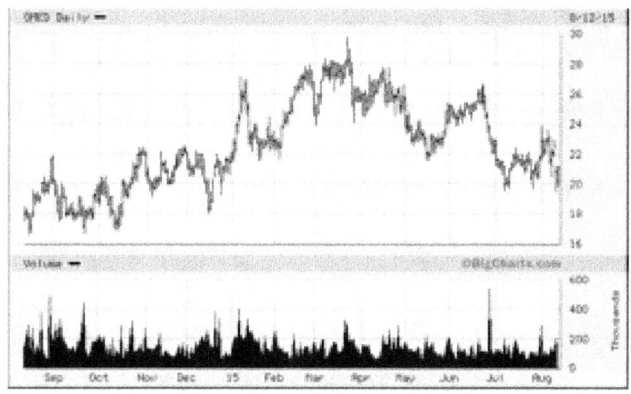

Stock price target: $40.

Financials: Cash of $ 213.05 million as of Q1, 2015.

Oncomed Therapeutics remains a top pick due to the broad pipeline and various strategic collaborations, which show confidence in its product pipeline.

TRACON Pharmaceuticals (TCON, NASDAQ)

TRACON Pharmaceuticals, Inc. is focused on the development and commercialization of novel targeted therapeutics for cancer, age-related macular degeneration and fibrotic diseases. The company is a leader in the field of endoglin biology.

Pipeline:

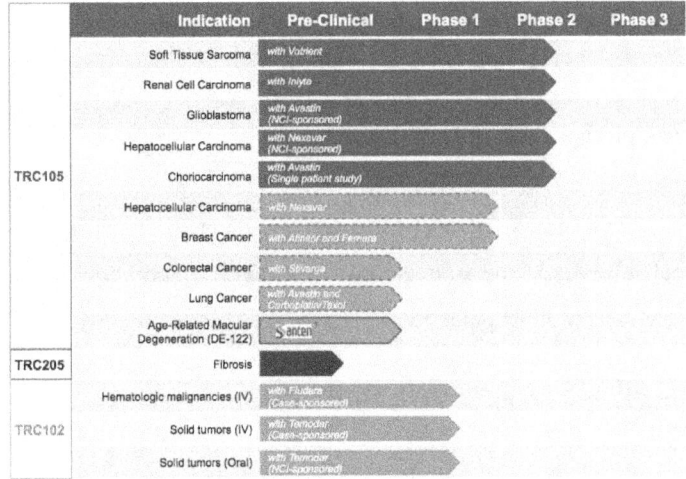

(Image adapted from the company's website)

The company's lead product candidate, TRC105, is an anti-endoglin antibody that is being developed for the treatment of multiple solid tumor types in combination with inhibitors of the VEGF pathway. TRC105 has orphan-drug designation in choriocarcinoma and sarcoma (phase 2 results expected in second half of 2015). It is

66

also in preclinical stage in age-related macular degeneration and other eye diseases in partnership with Santeen, the global ophthalmology company. Other product candidates are TRC205, an anti-endoglin antibody that is in preclinical development for the treatment of fibrotic diseases (with potential in non-alcoholic fibroproliferative diseases, renal fibrosis, interstitial pulmonary fibrosis, hypertrophic cardiomyopathy and end-stage pulmonary artery hypertension). The drug was shown to reverse fibrosis and improve survival in mice in preclinical studies. TRC102 is a small molecule that is in clinical development for the treatment of lung cancer and glioblastoma.

Partnerships: National Cancer Institute (TRC105, TRC102), Pfizer (PF03446962), Acceleron (Dalantercept), Santen (TRC105 in ophthalmology).

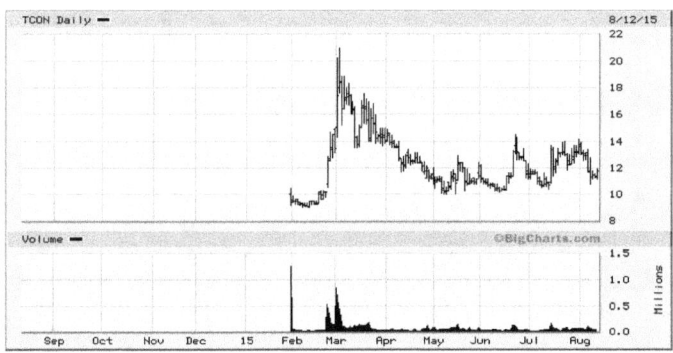

Stock Price target: $20.

Financials: $ 61.16M, Q1 2015.

NEA Management Company, the largest venture capital firm in the world owns 15.6 percent of the outstanding shares of TCON.

TRACON fits in our investment philosophy with a broad pipeline with potential across various disease classes and key collaborations with larger biotechnology/pharmaceutical companies.

Merrimack Pharmaceuticals (MACK, NASDAQ)

Merrimack Pharmaceuticals has two areas of focus in oncology therapeutics- tumor antibodies and nanotherapeutics (chemotherapy drugs encapsulated in liposomes that specifically target tumor cells).

Pipeline:

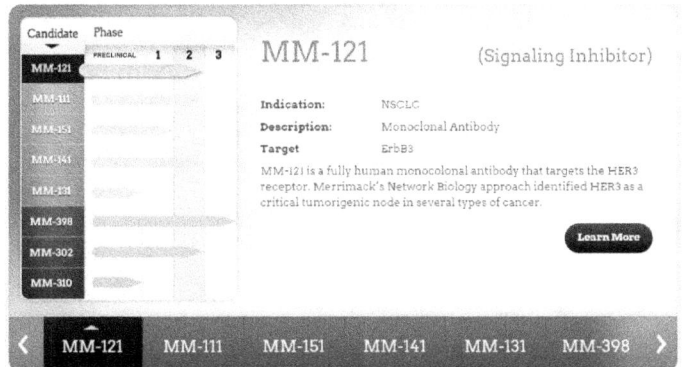

(Image adapted from the company's website)

MM-121 is a human monoclonal antibody that targets the HER3 receptor. Phase 2 trials have been completed in breast cancer, ovarian cancer, and lung cancer in combination with other drugs.

MM-398 is liposomal-encapsulated irinotecan with orphan drug designation in metastatic pancreatic cancer. The drug showed a significant improvement in overall survival in refractory metastatic pancreatic cancer in phase 3 trial and is pending FDA review in October, 2015. The drug is also being tested in malignant glioma and colorectal cancer.

MM-111 is a first-in-class biospecific antibody targeting HER2 and HER3 expressing tumor cells and being tested in an on-going phase 2 trial in gastric cancer.

MM-151 has three monoclonal antibodies targeting EGFR receptor in ongoing phase 1 trial in solid tumors like cancers of colon, non-small cell lung cancer and triple negative breast cancer.

Partnerships: Baxalta, Inc. (subsidiary of Baxter International).

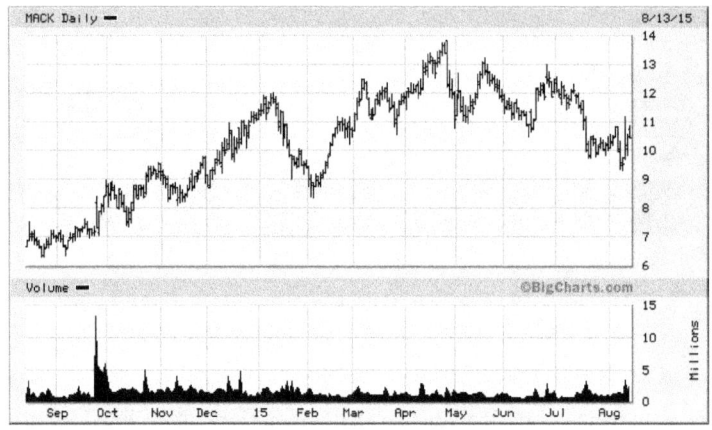

Stock Price target: $ 15

Financials: Cash of $ 91.7 million as of Q1, 2015.

Merrimack Pharmaceuticals is one of the top three picks of JPMorgan for 2015 with a price target of $15.

Celldex Therapeutics (CLDX, NASDAQ)

The company's pipeline is comprised of therapeutic antibodies, antibody drug conjugates, immune system modulators and vaccines. The pipeline has candidates in 2 pivotal trials in brain cancer and triple negative breast cancer.

Pipeline:

CANDIDATE	INDICATION	Preclinical	Phase 1	Phase 2	Phase 3
RINTEGA	Front-line GBM	ACT IV Registration Trial (EGFRvIII)			
	Recurrent GBM	ReACT Trial (EGFRvIII)			
Glembatumumab Vedotin	TNBC	METRIC Trial (gpNMB)			
	Metastatic Melanoma	(gpNMB)			
Varlilumab	Lym/Leu/Solid Tumors	(CD27)			
	Multiple Solid Tumors	+nivolumab (with BMS)			
	Metastatic Melanoma	+ipilimumab; CDX-1401			
	Renal Cell Carcinoma	+sunitinib			
CDX-1401	Metastatic Melanoma	+CDX-301 (NY-ESO-1) *IST			
CDX-301	HSCT	+Mozobil (FLT3L Pathway)			
	B-cell Lymphomas	+Rituxan *IST			

All programs wholly owned by Celldex   *Investigator sponsored trial

RINTEGA, the key product candidate has breakthrough designation for EGFR*vIII* positive glioblastoma (GBM) and is being tested in both front-line GBM and recurrent GBM. Phase 2 clinical trials showed significant improvements in both median progression-free survival and overall survival in newly diagnosed EGFR*vIII*-positive glioblastoma patients. The first interim analysis of phase 3 trial results of RINTEGA in newly diagnosed GBM was completed in June 2015 and the it was recommended to continue the study. The second interim analysis of the phase 3 study is expected to be completed in end of 2015 or early 2016. Investors did not like the news and the stock price has since fallen by more than 50 percent, however the decline represents an excellent entry point since the final data outcome is widely expected to be favorable.

Varlilumab is being tested in ongoing clinical studies with checkpoint inhibitors like nivolumab in multiple solid tumors. Three CDX-011 (Glembatumumab), an antibody-drug conjugate is being tested in an ongoing phase 3 trial with results expected in mid-2017. **Partnerships**: Bristol Myers Squibbs, Oncothyreon, Roche

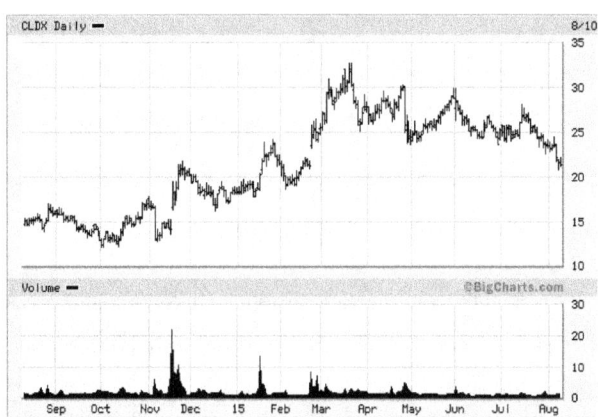

Stock price target: $ 38.

Financials: Cash of $ 360 million, Q1, 2015.

Cancer Companies with Targeted Therapies

Array Biopharma (ARRY, NASDAQ)

Array Biopharma is a biopharmaceutical company focused on development of small molecule oncology drugs (targeted cancer therapies). The company has six phase 3 studies in progress at the present.

Pipeline:

Product (Partner)	Phase
Binimetinib / MEK162 Indication: Cancer Target: MEK	Phase 3
Encorafenib / LGX818 Indication: Cancer Target: BRAF	Phase 3
Selumetinib (AstraZeneca) Indication: Cancer Target: MEK	Phase 3
Filanesib / ARRY-520 Indication: Multiple Myeloma Target: KSP	Phase 2
ARRY-797 Indication: LMNA related DCM Target: p38	Phase 2
ARRY-502 Indication: Asthma Target: CRTH2	Phase 2
Ipatasertib / GDC-0068 (Genentech) Indication: Cancer Target: AKT	Phase 2
Motolimod / VTX2337 (VentiRx / Celgene) Indication: Cancer Target: TLR	Phase 2
ASLAN001 / ARRY-543 (ASLAN) Indication: Cancer Target: Pan-HER	Phase 2
Danoprevir (InterMune/Roche) Indication: Hepatitis C Target: NS3 Protease	Phase 2
LY2606368 (Eli Lilly) Indication: Cancer Target: Chk-1	Phase 2
ARRY-614 Indication: MDS Target: p38/Tie2	Phase 1
ONT-380 (Oncothyreon) Indication: Breast Cancer Target: HER-2	Phase 1
GDC-0575 (Genentech) Indication: Cancer Target: Chk-1	Phase 1
LOXO-101 (Loxo Oncology) Indication: Cancer Target: PanTrk	Phase 1
GDC-0994 (Genentech) Indication: Cancer Target: ERK	Phase 1

As shown in the above figure, the company's strength is its wide pipeline of products which has won partnerships with other companies like Astra Zeneca, Genentech, Celgene, Oncothyreon, Roche, Eli Lilly and Loxo Oncology.

The company's shares jumped in January 2015 on the decision to acquire rights to Encorafenib from Novartis.. Array Biopharma has also developed a proprietary kinase inhibitors cleaning platform to generate new drug leads.

Results of phase 3 trial for Binimetinib are expected in 2016. Results of phase 3 trial in uveal melanoma are also expected in 2016.

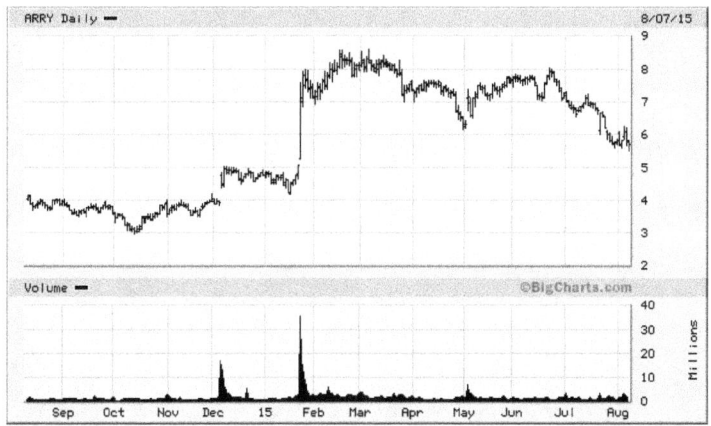

Stock Price target: $15

Management: The Company has an excellent management team and the CEO, who has an MBA from Kellogg University has past experience in senior management positions at Hospira and the oncology division at Pfizer.

Of note is the fact that 4% of outstanding shares are held by the prominent hedge fund, Baker Brothers.

Array biopharma is a key long-term investment supported by its wide pipeline of products, excellent management team and partnerships/collaborations. The stock has significant upside from its current price.

Mirati Therapeutics (MRTX, NASDAQ)

The company's area of focus in oncology is developing targeted therapies.

Pipeline:

CANDIDATE/INDICATION	PRIMARY TARGETS	PRE CLINICAL	PHASE I	PHASE 1B-PHASE 2	REGISTRATION TRIAL
KINASE PROGRAMS					
MGCD265 NSCLC	MET Axl				
MGCD265 Solid Tumors					
MGCD516 Solid Tumors	Trk RET DDR				
EPIGENETIC PROGRAMS					
Mocetinostat Bladder	HDAC 1,2,3,11				
Mocetinostat DLBCL					

(Image adapted from the company's website)

Tyrosine Kinase inhibitors are enzymes that play a key role in cell differentiation and abnormal signaling of this enzyme may be associated with abnormal tumor growth. Mirati's tyrosine kinase inhibitor, MGCD265 showed significant anti-tumor activity in a number of tumor models, with additional antitumor activity when combined with other anticancer agents like EGFR inhibitors. MET expression in non-small cell lung cancer (NSCLC) is associated with poor clinical outcome and is seen in about 3-4% of NSCLC patients. MGCD265 showed more than 90 percent inhibition of targets in phase 1 study in NSCLC. MGCD265 can also help to overcome EGFR resistance in NSCLC.

Mirati's other area of focus is epigenetic alterations in cancer that help to control gene expression. Mocetinostat is a spectrum selective Histone-Deacetylase (HDAC) inhibitor being tested in ongoing phase 1b / 2 trials in bladder cancer and diffuse large B cell lymphoma. In addition, Mocetinostat may also enhance the expression of checkpoint inhibitors like anti-PD1 and anti-PDL1 inhibitors and thus, may be useful in combination therapy with these immuno-oncology agents. Non-small cell lung cancer is one area where this combination may be clinically useful.

Partnerships:

Mirati Therapeutics has partnered with MedImmune, the global biologics research and development arm of AstraZeneca, to conduct a phase I/II study of mocetinostat, in combination with MedImmune's investigational anti-PD-L1 immune checkpoint inhibitor, durvalumab (MEDI4736) in non-small cell lung cancer with potential to explore for other indications in the future.

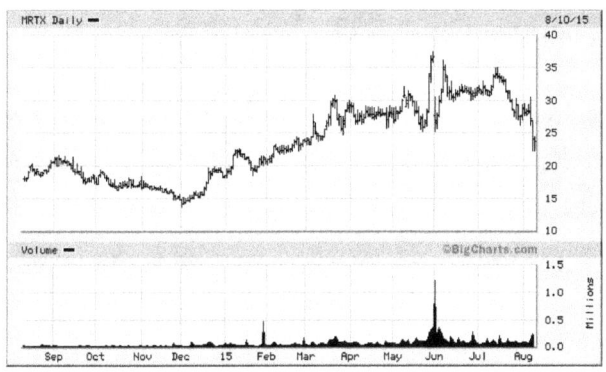

Stock price target: $42.

Financials: Cash of $68.02 million as of Q1, 2015.

Management: The Company's management includes scientists with experience in developing blockbuster kinase inhibitors like sunitinib in renal cell cancer and academic experience at MD Anderson Cancer Center.

Ownerships by key hedge funds: Baker Brothers: 17.3 % of outstanding as of Q1, 2015; Orbimed Advisors: 7.83 percent of outstanding shares as of Q1, 2015.

Nektar Therapeutics (NKTR, NASDAQ)

Nektar Therapeutics is a clinical-stage biopharmaceutical company with a product pipeline consists of drug candidates across a number of therapeutic areas, including oncology, pain, anti-infectives, anti-viral and immunology.

Pipeline:

(Image adapted from the company's website)

The company's pipeline is impressive and quite broad-based in different product categories. Naloxegol, the marketed product for opioid-induced constipation has a potential market of 38 million chronic pain patients in the U.S. NKTR-181 is an abuse deterrent opioid and has a fast track designation from the FDA in phase-3 trials. In its oncology pipeline, NKTR-214 is an immuno-oncology product candidate and has a potential to combine with checkpoint inhibitors.

Partnerships: Nektar therapeutics has key collaborations with AstraZeneca, Bayer, Baxter and MD Anderson Cancer Center.

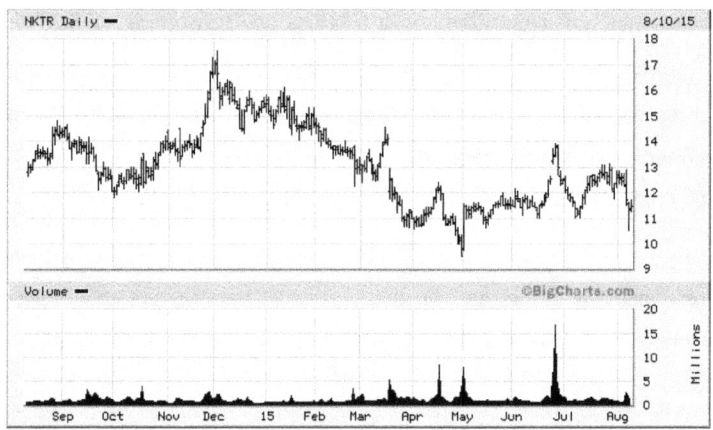

Stock price target: $ 25.

Financials: Cash of $ 300.8 million as of Q1, 2015.

Ariad Pharmaceuticals (ARIA, NASDAQ)

Ariad Pharmaceuticals has a marketed product, Iclusig (Ponatinib), a tyrosine kinase inhibitor which is approved in treatment of Philadelphia chromosome positive leukemias (chronic, accelerated, blast phase, Ph+ acute lymphocytic leukemia). The stock price took a hit in 2013 after reports of vascular occlusion resulting in arterial and venous thrombosis, including fatal myocardial infarction, stroke etc. surfaced. The sales of Iclusig were initially halted in 2013 but since then have picked up after clinicians are using it as a third line drug in chronic myelocytic leukemia (CML). A clinical trial testing Iclusig as a 3rd line therapy in CML is due to open in mid-2015. Another randomized phase 2 trial testing Iclusig as a second line drug in CML is being started in second half of 2015. Brigatinib is a potential best in the class oral ALK targeting tyrosine kinase inhibitor being tested in an ongoing phase 2 trial in refractory ALK+ non-small cell lung cancer. Preliminary results showed 74% objective response rate and tumor shrinkage in 100% patients in the data presented at ASCO 2015. The study is expected to be completed in November 2016 and the drug is expected to have a potential $ 2 billion dollar market by 2020. AP32788 is a new product candidate in preclinical studies in non-small cell lung cancer.

Pipeline:

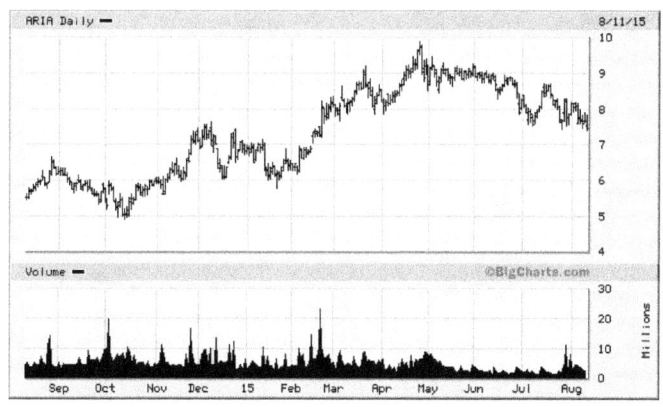

	PRECLINICAL	PROOF OF CONCEPT	PIVOTAL	APPROVED

Iclusig® (ponatinib)

CML, Ph+ ALL (refractory)

Ph+ ALL (with chemo, 1st, 2nd line)

AML (FLT3)

Lung cancer (FGFR)

Lung cancer (RET)

Gastrointestinal stromal tumors (KIT)

Medullary thyroid cancer (RET)

Biliary cancer (FGFR)

Brigatinib (AP26113)

Non-small cell lung cancer (ALK)

AP32788

Non-small cell lung cancer

(Image adapted from the company's website)

Partnerships: MD Anderson Cancer Center.

Stock price target: $ 15

Financials: The revenue projection is $ 130 million in 2015 and $ 400 million in 2018 (with no exchange to current Iclusig label). An

83

additional second line in CML indication might more than double Iclusig-generated revenue.

Sarissa Capital Management, an activist hedge fund (owns 6.9 percent of outstanding shares) is involved in an ongoing proxy battle with Ariad Pharmaceuticals. The management team comprises world class scientists who have been well published in prominent journals like Cell, Science etc. The current CEO, Harvey Berger, MD is an ex-academic at Emory University, University of Pennsylvania and Yale University and is due to retire by end of 2015 as a result of the ongoing proxy fight. Ariad has been considered a potential buyout target due to the value of its pipeline.

Dicerna Pharmaceuticals (DRNA, NASDAQ)

Dicerna's pipeline of drugs uses RNA interference or RNAi. Rather than targeting and binding to proteins to inhibit their activity like most drugs, RNAi exerts its effects one step earlier in the gene silencing process by targeting the mRNA. By targeting mRNA, RNAi can even target disease-causing target genes that are expressed exclusively inside cells and thus, cannot be reached by traditional antibody and small molecule technology.

Pipeline:

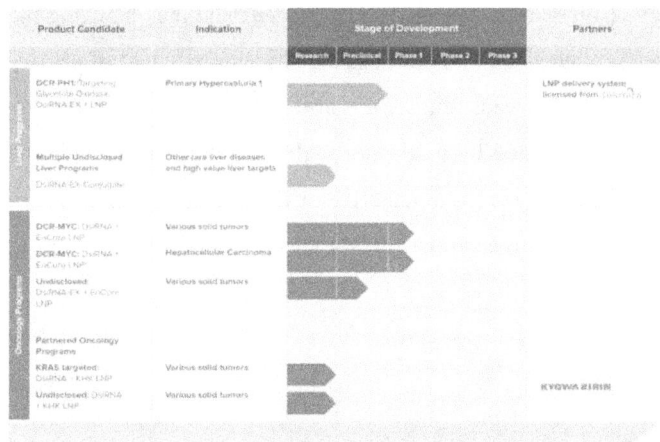

(Image adapted from the company's website)

Dicerna's oncology program involves targeting solid tumors expressing MYC oncogene. MYC oncogene acts as 'universal amplifier' in several oncogenic processes and is often considered an 'undruggable' target. The drug is being tested in phase 1b/2a studies in pancreatic neuroendocrine tumor and hepatocellular cancer (with potential in breast cancer, hepatocellular cancer, small cell lung cancer, gastric cancer and colorectal cancer). Pancreatic neuroendocrine tumor has about 300 patient/year in the US and current therapies are not much effective. DCR-PH1 is another key program targeting Primary Hyperoxaluria (PH) which can result in liver and kidney cancer if untreated. PH is an ultra-rare disease with an expected incidence of 1-3 cases per million population and estimated 6500 patients in the US and European Union. Dicerna's technology is aimed at silencing the HAO1 gene and thus blocking the oxalate production. In animal studies, near normal level of urinary oxalate was observed. Studies are also being performed in undisclosed rare inherited liver diseases with about 5200 patients in the US and the EU. There is a potential for expanding the indication to nonalcoholic steatohepatitis, alpha-1 antitrypsin deficiency, etc.

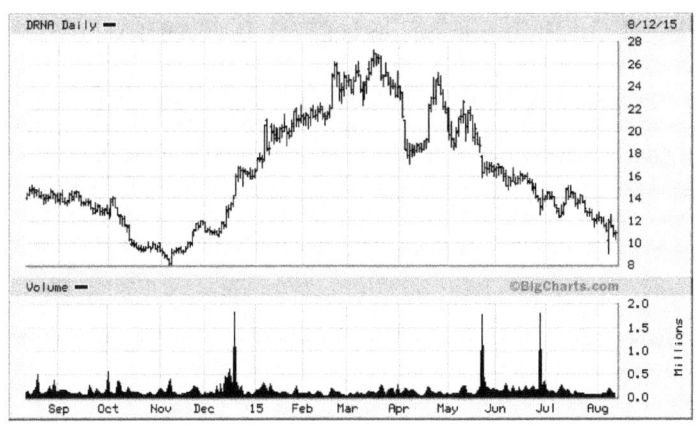

Stock Price target: $ 30.

Financials: Cash of $ 87 million as of Q1, 2015.

About 13.6% of the float is held by the prominent hedge fund RA Capital with an expected value of $ 58 million.

Threshold Pharmaceuticals (THLD, NASDAQ)

Thresold Pharmaceuticals' key product, Evofosfamide, is activated by tumor hypoxia and is being tested in two pivotal phase 3 trials, first one in pancreatic cancer (orphan drug designation) and soft tissue sarcoma (orphan drug designation, results expected early 2016). Encouraging phase -2 data of the drug in multiple myeloma was presented earlier in 2015. In addition, [18F]-HX4 is a hypoxia Positron Emission Tomography (PET) imaging agent being developed as a potential diagnostic aid in the company's tumor hypoxia product pipeline.

Pipeline:

TRIAL	DESCRIPTION	PHASE	
THERAPEUTICS: TH-302			
TH-CR-406	Soft Tissue Sarcoma	3	›
MAESTRO	Pancreatic Cancer	3	›
TH-CR-415	Non-squamous Non-small Cell Lung Cancer	2	›
TH-CR-413	Advanced Melanoma	2	›
TH-CR-408	Multiple Myeloma	1/2	›
TH-IST-4003	Astrocytoma	1/2	›
TH-IST-4004	RCC, HCC	1/2	›
TH-CR-407	Advanced Leukemias	1	›
TH-CR-410	RCC, GIST, PNET	1	›
TH-IST-4001	Various Solid Tumors	1	›
THERAPEUTICS: TH-4000			
TH-CR-601	Non-Small Cell Lung Cancer	2	›
TH-CR-602	Head & Neck Squamous Cell Carcinoma	2	›
DIAGNOSTICS: [18F]-HX4			
[18F]-HX4	Various Solid Tumors	2	›

Tumor Hypoxia:

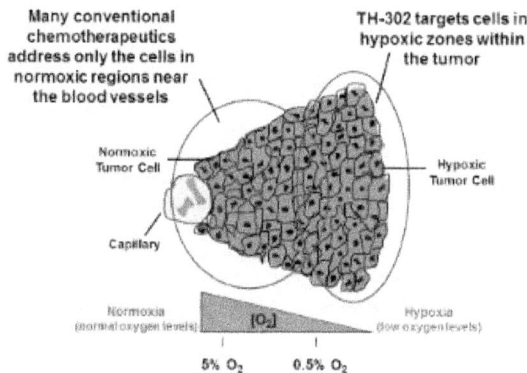

Many conventional chemotherapeutics address only the cells in normoxic regions near the blood vessels

TH-302 targets cells in hypoxic zones within the tumor

Normoxic Tumor Cell

Hypoxic Tumor Cell

Capillary

Normoxia (normal oxygen levels)

[O₂]

Hypoxia (low oxygen levels)

5% O₂   0.5% O₂

(Images adapted from the company's website.)

Tumor hypoxia has a key role in tumor progression, metastasis, and resistance to radiotherapy and standard chemotherapy. Targeting areas of tumor hypoxia is thus a promising therapeutic approach.

Partnerships: Merck KGaA for Evofosfamide.

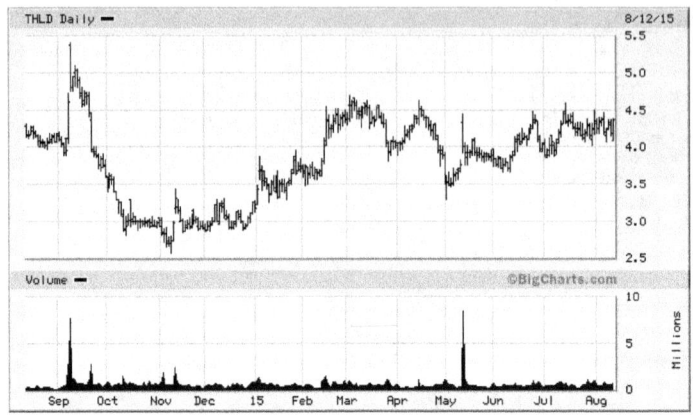

Stock Price target: $ 12.

Financials: Cash of $ 78.89 million as of Q1, 2015.

The company's management is excellent and the CEO, Harold Selick, PhD is an expert in humanized antibody therapeutics. The Chief Scientific Officer, Mark Matteucci was the first scientist at Gilead and is the co-inventor of DNA synthesis technology, the foundation of modern gene medicine.

The notable hedge fund, Baker Brothers own 4.1% stake in THLD. Other competitors in tumor hypoxia space include Novacea (acquired) and Proacta, a private company. This leaves THLD as the only public company in tumor hypoxia space.

The stock hit a high of $9 in 2012 and has retraced since after the results of a stage 2 trial in pancreatic cancer showed no improvement in overall survival although progression-free survival improved significantly. At its current price, the company's stock provides an attractive buying opportunity.

Epizyme (EPZM, NASDAQ)

Epizyme is a clinical stage biotechnology company with its product candidate pipeline consisting of small molecule inhibitors of a class of enzymes known as histone methyltransferases, or HMTs. Genetic alterations can result in changes to the activity of HMTs, making them oncogenic. Inhibition of HMTs may impact gene expression and could be therapeutic in various cancers.

Pipeline:

Product Candidate	Clinical Populations	Stage of Development	Commercial Rights	Diagnostic Collaborator
EPZ-6438 (EZH2 inhibitor)	Non-Hodgkin lymphomas, including germinal center diffuse large B-cell lymphoma and follicular lymphoma as well as non-germinal center DLBCL, including primary mediastinal B-cell lymphoma (EZH2)	Phase 1/2 clinical trial ongoing • Phase 1 dose escalation complete; Phase 1 dose expansion enrolling at the highest two tested dose levels • Phase 2 trial for expanded population of non-Hodgkin lymphoma patients expected to initiate in the second quarter of 2015	Epizyme: Worldwide rights, ex-Japan Eisai: Japan	Roche: (Non-Hodgkin lymphoma with EZH2 point mutations)
	Other solid tumors such as synovial sarcoma and MRT (INI1-deficient)	Phase 1 trial for pediatric patients with INI1-deficient tumors, including MRT, expected to initiate in the second half of 2015 Phase 2 trial for adult patients with INI1-deficient tumors, including synovial sarcoma, expected to initiate in the second half of 2015 Clinical pharmacology studies evaluating food effects and drug/drug interactions expected to initiate in 2015		None - existing standard of care immunohistoch emical testing used at time of diagnosis to be utilized for studies in INI1-deficient tumors

Product Candidate	Clinical Populations	Stage of Development	Commercial Rights	Diagnostic Collaborator
EPZ-5676 (DOT1L inhibitor)	Acute leukemias with alterations in the *MLL* gene • MLL-r subtype of acute myeloid leukemia, or AML, and acute lymphoblastic leukemia, or ALL, in adult patients (Chromosomal translocation involving the *MLL* gene) • MLL-r in pediatric patients (Chromosomal translocation involving the *MLL* gene)	Phase 1 MLL-r adult patient trial ongoing • Dose escalation fully enrolled in MLL-r adult patient trial • MLL-r only adult expansion enrolling Phase 1 MLL-r pediatric patient trial enrolling	Epizyme: United States Celgene: Rest of world	None - existing standard of care molecular testing used at time of diagnosis to be utilized for studies in MLL-r leukemia

(Image adapted from the company's website.)

Partnerships: Celgene (EPZ-5676), GlaxoSmithkline (EPZ-5676), Eisai (EPZ-5676).

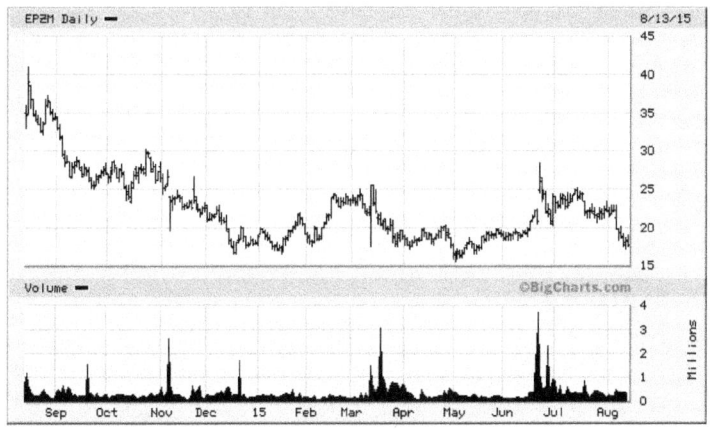

Stock Price target: $ 40

Financials: Cash of $ 244.5 million as of Q1, 2015.

The stock has multiple near-time catalysts. Phase 1 data of EPZ-5676 in adult and pediatric leukemia is expected in late 2015. Preliminary phase 2 data of EPZ-6438 is expected in mid-2016. The company's management is excellent and the CEO Robert Gould has 20 years of experience at Merck.

NEA Management, LLC, the large venture capital firm owns 12.5 percent of Epizyme's outstanding shares.

Loxo Oncology (LOXO, NASDAQ)

Loxo Oncology's is developing multiple small molecule therapeutics with specific cancer targets. Its lead compound in Phase 1 development, LOXO-101, is the only selective TRK inhibitor currently in clinical development. The company also has pre-clinical programs in development, through its collaboration with Array BioPharma, for RET, FGFR, and FLT3.

Pipeline: LOXO-101, a selective inhibitor of Trk family of tyrosine kinase inhibitors is in phase 1 trials in multiple tumor types including lung, head and neck, salivary, neuroblastoma, melanoma, colorectal cancer and breast cancer. Trk may join mutations like EGFR, ALK, BRAF and RET as one of the effective targeted cancer therapies.

In preclinical studies, the drug exhibited tumor inhibition across various tumor types. Results of phase 1, dose escalation and safety study are expected in end of 2015 or early 2016. In the preliminary phase 1 data presented at ASCO 2015, the drug was generally well tolerated in 15 patients.

Loxo Oncology also has other compounds in development including RET-inhibitor, Fibroblast Growth Factor Inhibitor, and FMS like tyrosine kinase inhibitor (may be useful in AML).

Other competitors in the Trk inhibitor space include Mirati Therapeutics, Tesaro and Novartis but LOXO-101 is the most selective Trk inhibitor of these.

Partnerships with larger companies: Array Biopharma.

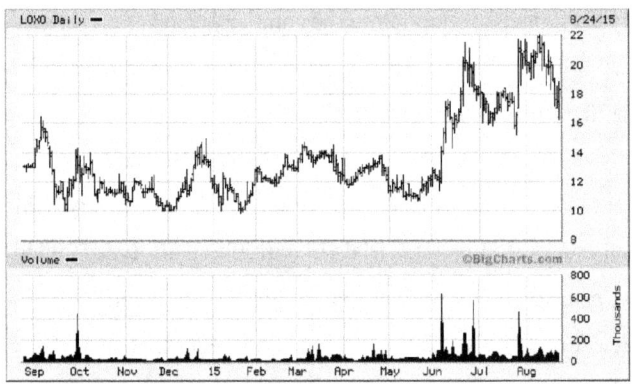

Stock Price Target: $ 25

Financials: Cash of $ 107.6 Millions as of Q1, 2015, enough to last till 2017.

Loxo has excellent management and scientific advisors from prominent academic institutions like Massachusetts General Hospital, Memorial Sloan Kettering Hospital, John Hopkins University and National Cancer Institute. NEA Management Company holds 10.7% of the outstanding stock float.

Aduro Biotech (ADRO, NASDAQ)

Aduro Biotech is a recent IPO whose LADD-based platform technology is a cancer vaccine using Listeria Monocytogenes bacteria which are modified to express specific tumor antigens. The modified bacteria are injected in the patient whose dendritic cells absorb the bacteria and launch immune response specific to the tumor. In addition, the company owns the rights to GVAX, which is a portfolio of irradiated tumor cell lines that express GM-CSF, a key immune cell recruitment factor, and can launch a potent immune response.

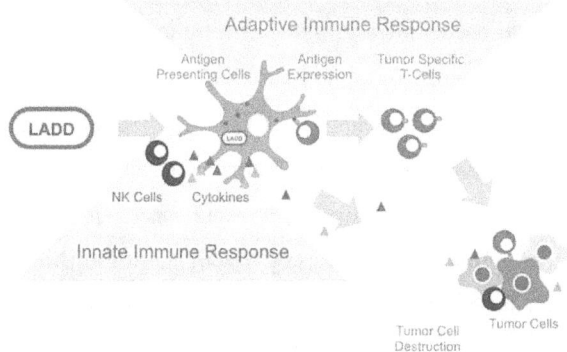

(Image adapted from the company website)

Pipeline:

CRS-207: LADD-technology based product designed to express mesothelin, which is expressed in various tumors, including pancreatic cancer. The combination of CRS-207 and GVAX has been granted breakthrough therapy designation in metastatic pancreatic

97

cancer. Based on promising results from the first phase 2 trial, Aduro is testing GVAX Pancreas (with low-dose cyclophosphamide) and CRS-207 compared to chemotherapy or to CRS-207 alone in previously treated pancreatic cancer. In addition, the combination of CRS-207 and GVAX is being tested in combination with Nivolumab (anti-PD1 immune check-point inhibitor from Bristol Myers) in metastatic pancreatic cancer.

Aduro's LADD-technology based molecules are also being tested in glioma (brain cancer), mesothelioma (associated with asbestos), lung cancer and prostate cancer.

The company's CDNs (cyclic dinucleotide) are small molecules which have been shown to induce strong immune response when injected in proximity to tumors and may be useful in combination with other anti-cancer agents.

Partnerships: The Company has partnerships with Janssen Biotech for using its LADD based platform in prostate cancer. It has also partnered with John Hopkins University researchers to further develop its LADD and DVAX based therapies. In addition, it has partnered with Novartis for development of CDN based immunotherapies.

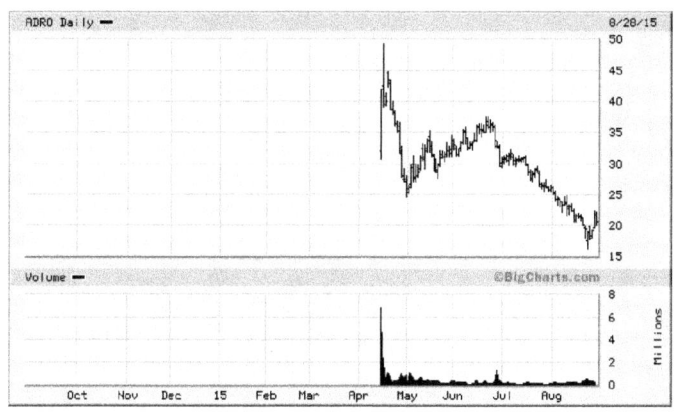

Stock Price Target: $45

Financials: Cash of $465.87M, Q1, 2015.

Major early investors include Morningside Ventures, a prominent venture capital firm, which holds >19 million shares.

CHAPTER 5

Going Beyond the Select List: Immune Check-point Inhibitors and Few Biotech Investing Pearls

As of the time of writing this chapter, Barron's magazine has published a cover article with the title 'The New Cure' discussing the biotechnology revolution in immune-oncology (Barron's, August 24, 2015). Though none of the immune checkpoint inhibitor companies made it to our select list (primarily since these companies have already appreciated a lot in their stock price and we felt that they do not meet our minimum 50% upside potential criteria), this book would be incomplete without mentioning these companies.

The biggest players in the immune-oncology field of check-point inhibitors are Bristol-Myers Squibb (BMY), Pfizer (PFE), Merck (MRK), Roche (ROG, Switzerland), and AstraZeneca (AZN). Bristol-Myers's anti-PD1 checkpoint inhibitor Opdivo (nivolumab) has shown impressive results in non-small cell lung cancer and malignant melanoma and is being tested in various other cancers like renal cell cancer, head/neck cancer and brain cancer (glioblastoma). Former U.S. President Jimmy Carter will receive Merck's anti-PD1 drug Keytruda (pembrolizumab) for metastatic melanoma. In my opinion, the best bet among these big players is Bristol-Myers Squibb with another 20% possible upside potential in the stock price.

Adaptive cell therapies like CAR-T are being tested in combination with immune check-point inhibitors. MedImmune (part of AstraZenca) is starting a phase 1b trial combining it anti-PDL1 antibody (PD-L1) MEDI4736 with Juno Therapeutics' anti-CD19 CAR-T therapy. New immune targets like indoleamine dioxygenase-1 (IDO1) inhibitors (for example, INCB24360 from Incyte Corporation, INCY) are being tested in combination with check-point inhibitors. Combinations of various cancer immune-therapies holds great promise in this area.

Few other promising emerging public companies in cancer therapy (which did not make it to our select list but could be researched further by investors) are listed below.

- Incyte Corporation (INCY, NASDAQ): The company's main product is Jakafi, JAK1/JK1 inhibitor, however we are more excited about the potential of its cancer immune-therapy, anti-IDO1 antibody which is being tested in melanoma, lung cancer and various other solid tumors. The company's stock had a huge run-up and investors are advised to wait for a lower entry-point.

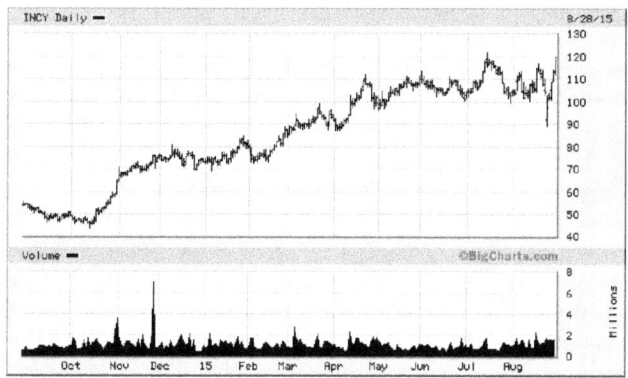

- <u>Atara Bio (ATRA, NASDAQ)</u>: Atara Bio's pipeline includes molecularly-targeted product candidates (targeting TGF-beta proteins myostatin and actin) and T-cell product candidates (targeting Epsteein-Barr Virus and Cytomegalovirus). The T cell product candidates are under clinical trials in various hematological malignancies. Boston based hedge fund, Baupost Group owns 19.74% of the stock float.

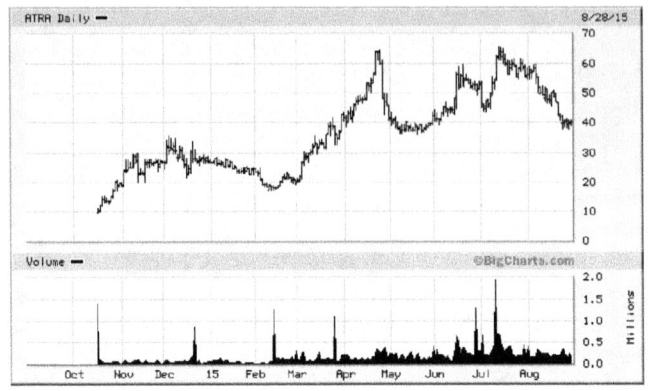

-Exelixis, Inc. (EXEL, NASDAQ): The key product in its pipeline is cabozantinib, a drug targeted at tyrosine kinases including MET, VEGF receptors, AXL, and RET. The drug is F.D.A. approved in the treatment of progressive, metastatic, medullary thyroid cancer. The company's stock took a big hit in 2015 when cabozantinib failed to meet its primary end-points in a phase 3 trial in prostate cancer. However, the stock has more than tripled from its lows after a successful phase 3 trial in metastatic renal cell cancer. The results of an on-going phase 3 trial of cabozantinib in liver cancer are expected in late 2016. In addition, cobimetinib (Roche/Genentech partnership), a MEK inhibitor had a successful phase 3 trial in malignant melanoma and is pending F.D.A approval. Exelixis is also being considered a buy-out candidate.

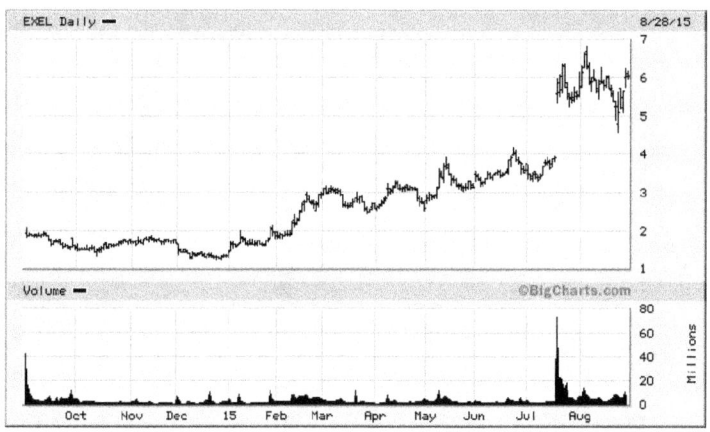

- ProNAi (DNAI, NASDAQ): This sis a recent IPO whose cancer therapies use its proprietary DNA interference program. Its lead product candidate, PNT2258 targets a cancer causing gene, BCL2 that is linked to various cancers. The molecule is being tested in an ongoing phase 2 trial in third-line refractory or relapsed diffuse large B-cell lymphoma and another phase 2 trial in Richter's syndrome is expected to begin this year.

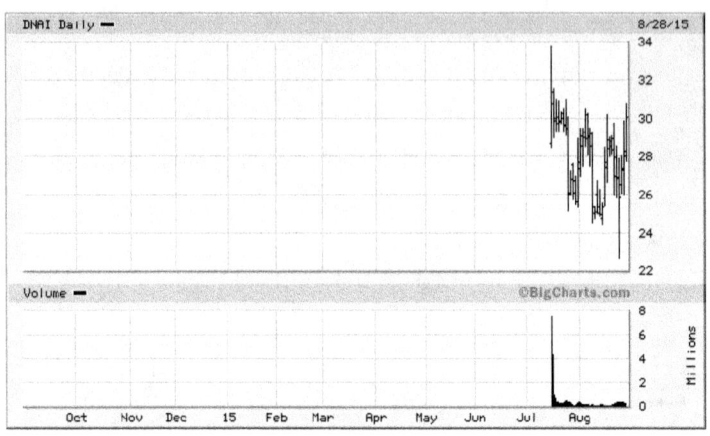

-Tesaro, Inc. (TSRO, NASDAQ): Its product pipeline consists of Rolapitant, which is pending F.D.A. approval in cancer chemotherapy-induced nausea and vomiting. In addition, Niraparib, a polymerase inhibitor is in phase 3 trials in ovarian cancer and breast cancer, and is being tested in combination with Merck's anti-PD1 Keytruda in ovarian cancer and triple negative breast cancer. Various other immunotherapies like anti-TIM-3 antibody, anti-LAG-3 antibody etc. are in early discovery stage.

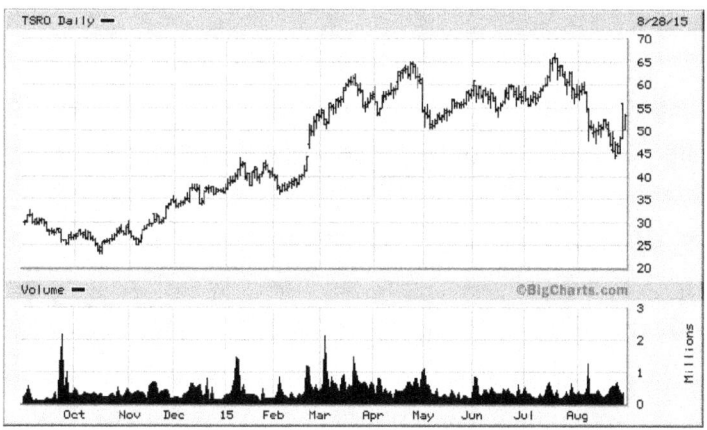

Immune Design (IMDZ, NASDAQ): The Company's immunother-apy pipeline includes tumor-specific T cells which can be modified to express specific tumor types. The products are being tested in phase 1 trials in various solid tumors. It has partnered with Roche in a combination trial of its immune boost agent, CMB305 with Roche's anti-PD-L1 drug, atezolizumab in soft tissue sarcoma.

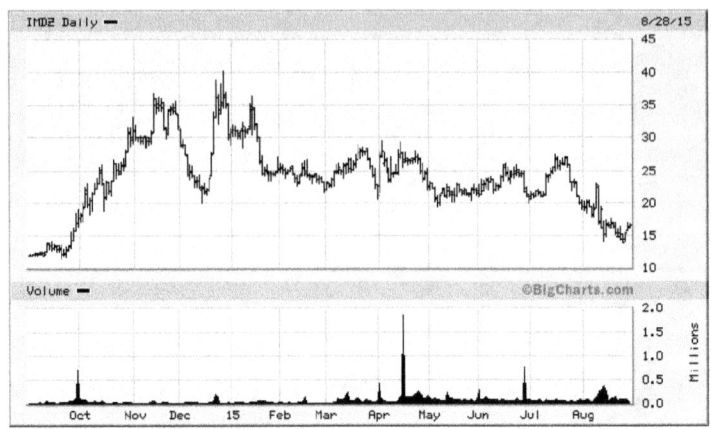

MacroGenics, Inc. (MGNX, NASDAQ): Its cancer monoclonal antibodies are in clinical trials in breast cancer and various solid tumors. Key collaborations include Janssen, Gilead, Servier, Pfizer and Boehringer Ingelheim.

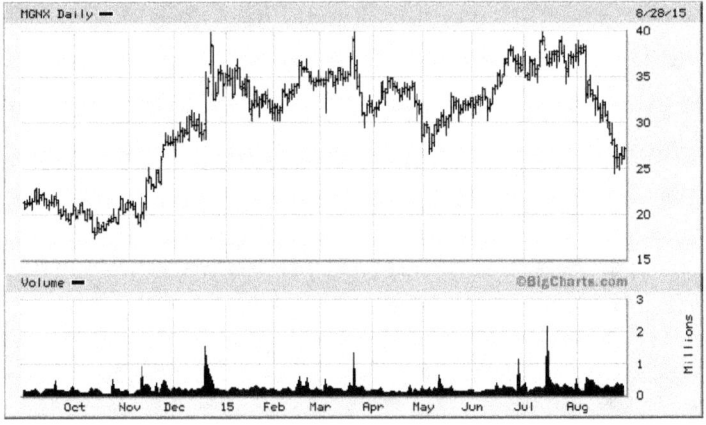

108

: I/we hold long positions in INCY, ATRA, EXEL, TSRO, MGNX, IMDZ, JUNO and DNAI. I/we have no positions in BMY, PFE, MRK, AZN and ROG.

A suggested portfolio allocation is be equal-weight distribution of above mentioned stocks in the select list in chapter 4. Among the stocks mentioned in chapter 5, I feel more optimistic about significant upside in ATRA, EXEL, IMDZ, MGNX and DNAI and suggest that investors take a close look at these companies.

Few Pearls of Biotechnology Investing:

Biotechnology stocks historically have been volatile with swings of 50 percent or more depending on the results of clinical trials. Even after FDA approval, the arrival of newer, more promising therapies can cause the stock price of a promising company to decline significantly from its highs. The buy-and-hold for years approach does not work very well in biotechnology investing in my opinion and investors need to be vigilant about their portfolio holdings. The reward of this vigilance is potential for multi-fold gains which outranks most other sectors in my opinion.

A suggested investing strategy is taking profits at key milestones achieved by the stock. For example, if the stock gains 50 percent in price, sell 25% of the initial investment. If the stock doubles, sell 35% of the original investment of shares. At this point, the investor has almost regained whole of his initial investment and still has 40% shares of the original investment which he should hold on in case the stock price multiplies many-fold and the stock goes on to be the next large-cap biotech company like Gilead or Illumina. This strategy helps to protect profits as well as keeps the margin open for the stock price to become a multi-bagger.

Few investors also try to play the upcoming catalysts like results of phase 3 trials. Depending on the results of earlier trials, the stock prices of companies may start getting a boost 6-9 months in advance of the expected data. However, most investors are quick in profit-taking after a huge-run up and sell in advance of the trial results. The expected completion date of a clinical trial is available by searching the company name and the disease at https://clinical-trials.gov. Conservative investors who want to avoid the wide swings in biotech stock prices may consider investing in exchange traded funds like my favorite, ALPS Medical Breakthroughs ETF (SBIO, NYSE).

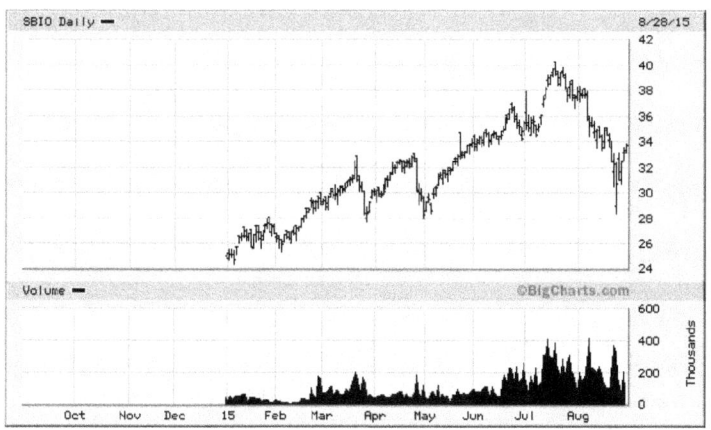

SBIO had a big run-up since its inception but has corrected in the recent sell-off and is offering an attractive entry point to investors.

Another promising swing trading strategy could be waiting for biotechnology ETFs like IBB and XBI to correct to slightly below their 200 day moving averages which has offered a support to the stock prices over last 3-4 years. Since I started investing in biotech space, I have seen two big sell-offs in this space (Jan-Feb 2012 and August 2015) and the stock prices of these ETFs found a support just below their 200 day simple moving averages. Most individual biotech stocks move in tandem with the market (unless they have an upcoming catalyst) and these support levels in key biotech ETFs may also serve as attractive buying points for other individual biotech stocks on an investor's watch list.

111

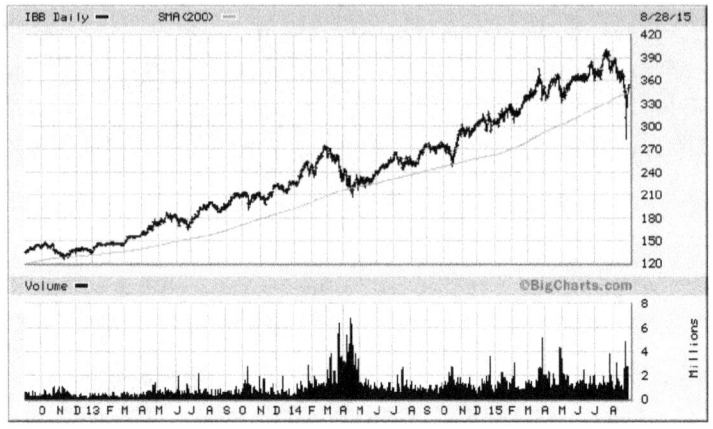

In conclusion, the biotechnology sector, especially the cancer treatment area is under a revolution now and is offering investors once-in a lifetime opportunity to gain and become rich from this revolution. The companies mentioned in this book have groundbreaking technologies which have the potential to bring new hope to millions of cancer patients and also offer the investors opportunity to achieve market-beating returns in their portfolio.

Bibiliography

1. Golec JH, Vernon JA. Financial Risk in the biotechnology Industry. 2007. Available at http://www.nber.org/papers/w13604

2. 2013 Biopharmaceutical Research Industry Profile – PhRMA. Available at:
http://www.phrma.org/sites/default/files/pdf/PhRMA%20Profile%202013.pdf

3. Available at: http://www.mdanderson.org/patient-and-cancer-information/cancer-information/clinical-trials/phases-of-clinical-trials/index.html

4. Available at: http://clincancerres.aacrjournals.org/content/18/24/6580/F1.large.jpg

5. Chimeric Antigen Receptor. Available at https://en.wikipedia.org/wiki/Chimeric_antigen_receptor

.

ABOUT THE AUTHOR

Dr. Bhavneesh Sharma, M.D., M.B.A. is a U.S. (Boston) based physician with American Board certifications in Pulmonary Diseases, Critical Care Medicine and Internal Medicine. He has over 15 years of clinical experience in various clinical settings. He did clinical training and research at prestigious medical institutes including Delhi University/ Maulana Azad Medical College (ranked second in India), Cornell University Medical College affiliated hospitals and Harvard University. He has been awarded the Young Investigator Award twice from the American College of Chest Physicians. He was awarded the National Research Service Award Research Fellowship at Harvard University by the National Institute of Health, Bethesda, Maryland. He was also selected among the top twenty Young Investigators in the U.S. in the field of Sleep Medicine by the American Academy of Sleep Medicine. He has several highly-cited peer reviewed publications in reputed medical journals like Chest and American College of Respiratory and Critical Care Medicine.

Apart from his expertise in the field of medicine, Dr. Bhavneesh Sharma has an M.B.A. with specialization in Finance and Financial Markets from the New York University's Stern School of Business (ranked first in finance in the U.S. in the LinkedIn M.B.A. rankings). He has navigated the financial markets for 8 years and has been investing exclusively in biotechnology/ health-care area for two years. He is also the owner/ investment manager of a start-up investment management firm, Vasuda Capital Management which operates a life sciences focused private investment fund, Vasuda Life Sciences Fund and also offers separate managed accounts for investors.

Dr. Sharma lives in Andover, Massachusetts in Boston suburbs with his wife and son and likes to travel, eat out or spend time with friends and family in spare time.

Contact Information:

Email: bhavn008@gmail.com

Notes